YOUR HOTLINE TO HAPPINESS

Imagine having the power within yourself to manifest extra money, luck, love, creativity, and a better self-image. You have the power to get what you want out of life. You simply need some celestial assistance.

Celestial 911 is your hotline to happiness. Once you learn how to call your guardian angel by wiring into your right brain, you will start to live the life you've always dreamed of.

The twenty-four guided Action Plans in this book will help you break through the left-brain static of limited belief and make a clear connection with the right brain. By performing these Action Plans, you will rewire yourself and reconnect with your original message of no limitations.

Pick up *Celestial 911* and make that call today. Your guardian angel is standing by to grant you unlimited wishes.

ABOUT THE AUTHOR

Robert B. Stone, Ph.D., is the author and co-author of over 80 published books, several with sales of over a million copies, as well as scores of magazine articles, most recently one in *Cosmopolitan*. He has lectured worldwide on human potential and was a past instructor at the University of Hawaii on activating the powers of the mind. A MENSA member, he has a degree from the Massachusetts Institute of Technology and was elected to the New York Academy of Science. A Silva Method lecturer for 20 years and Ambassador-at-Large for the Silva Method for 10 years, he introduced the Silva Method in Japan, New Zealand, India, the Soviet Union, and Thailand. Married to his wife Lola for 43 years, he lives in Hawaii and continues to help bring out the guru in others.

TO WRITE TO THE AUTHOR

If you wish to contact the author or would like more information about this book, please write to the author in care of Llewellyn Worldwide and we will forward your request. Both the author and publisher appreciate hearing from you and learning of your enjoyment of this book and how it has helped you. Llewellyn Worldwide cannot guarantee that every letter written to the author can be answered, but all will be forwarded. Please write to:

Robert B. Stone, Ph.D.
℅ Llewellyn Worldwide
P.O. Box 64383, Dept. K697-1
St. Paul, MN 55164-0383, U.S.A.

Please enclose a self-addressed stamped envelope for reply, or $1.00 to cover costs. If outside U.S.A., enclose international postal reply coupon.

CELESTIAL 911

CALL WITH YOUR RIGHT
BRAIN FOR ANSWERS!

Robert B. Stone, Ph.D.

1997
Llewellyn Publications
St. Paul, Minnesota 55164-0383, U.S.A.

FIRST EDITION
First Printing, 1997

Cover art by Geoff Smith/Scott Hull Associates
Cover design by Anne Marie Garrison
Editing and book design by Rebecca Zins

Permission to quote and use Silva Method material is kindly
granted from José Silva and Silva International, Inc.

Library of Congress Cataloging-in-Publication Data
Stone, Robert B.
 Celestial 911: call with your right brain for answers! /
Robert B. Stone.—1st ed.
  p. cm.
 Includes bibliographical references.
 ISBN 1-56718-697-1 (pbk.)
 1. Guides (Spiritualism)   I. Title.
BF1275.G85S75 1997
131—dc21   97–18540
                                                           CIP

Llewellyn Publications
A Division of Llewellyn Worldwide, Ltd.
P.O. Box 64383, Dept. K697-1
St. Paul, MN 55164-0383, U.S.A.

A word of sincere thanks
to my wife Lola for her support;
to my super typist Joanne Spletter
for her backup;
and to my editor Rebecca Zins
for her understanding and skill.

CONTENTS

ACTION PLANS

PREFACE

Fairy tales are real. The reason we do not accept them as real is because they appear to have no identifiable place in the real or material world.

But they do have a place in the non-material world. What earthly good is the non-material world? Every earthly good! It is the source of the material world, of the Earth itself.

Humanity has not acquired a language that applies to the non-material world. So the creative realm—free of time, space, or shape—is an indescribable realm due to a lack of vocabulary. All we have to rely on are angels and fairies.

Seers and philosophers speak in parables. They rely on magic, myths, and monsters—figments of the imagination.

Hold it right there. Angels and fairies are real!

Scientists have recently discovered that relaxed imaging activates the right hemisphere of the brain. This brain hemisphere is capable of creativity, of genius-like solutions, of transcending time and space, of manifesting miraculously the "figments" of the imagination.

How the right brain does this is the most remarkable accomplishment totally unexplainable by any language. But it is made quite understandable by the language of myths and fairy tales.

Here now is a fairy tale that opens the door to making all fairy tales come true.

1

HOW TO CONTACT THE GOOD FAIRY WAITING TO GRANT YOUR UNLIMITED WISHES

You have been attracted to these pages because you are ready to benefit from them. This works as surely as the law of gravity. The law of gravity is a physical law. The law of attraction is a metaphysical law. You can see the law of gravity work every time. But with a metaphysical law like the law of attraction, now you see it, now you don't.

It is the "don't" part that drives scientists crazy. So they stick with physical laws and pay no attention to laws beyond the physical.

On the other hand, you are now being exposed to the non-physical laws that symbolically involve good fairies, angels, genies, and wizards because you have lived your life in a certain way.

Let's look at a couple of possible ways that you make yourself eligible for this help that comes from the other side of our physical world.

In *The Wizard of Oz*, Dorothy was in a position where she needed help and she needed it now. She expressed that need. The Good Witch quickly appeared and filled Dorothy's need. What made Dorothy eligible? Obviously her innocence. She was guileless. She had no motives behind her motives.

In *Cinderella*, the good fairy appeared and enabled Cinderella to thwart her evil sisters. That's because Cinderella was obviously good. The fairy tale brings out her goodness right from the start.

You have some positive quality that makes you deserving of similar help. This means that you have the equivalent of a good fairy waiting to grant your wishes —not one or three or ten, but unlimited wishes.

In this chapter, you will contact this power and begin the flow of "good luck" that it appears to be.

Although fairy-tale language helps to explain help from the invisible realm, the help itself is no fairy tale. It is the very energy of creation itself, using you and me as co-creators.

It enables you to:

- Get as much money as you need.
- Increase your attractiveness to other people.
- Reap a crop of good luck every day.
- Revitalize your health and even postpone aging.
- Protect yourself from those who are "out to get you."
- Climb the ladder to social, business or political success.
- Buy and sell at the right time.
- Affect events at a distance.

The genie gave Aladdin three wishes. He did not limit the kind of wishes Aladdin could choose. Nor are any limits imposed on you as you lock into the limitless creative realm and activate its colossal power.

THE SCIENTIFIC NATURE OF THIS FAIRY-TALE APPROACH

The use of fairy-tale language, references to fantasy and symbolism, and writing in parables may give some readers the idea that this author is flaky.

Let us put such suspicions to rest. I have had over seventy-five books published in the fields of self-help and using more of the mind. There are millions of copies in print in fifteen languages. I am a graduate of the Massachusetts Institute of Technology, a member of MENSA (top 2% IQ in the world), and have been elected to the New York Academy of Sciences.

It is difficult for me to recall that I was not always as fluent as I am now—that I once was a socially deprived, bashful, retiring, shy, and silent child.

But I have a good fairy.

Because of my scientific background, you are likely to applaud the occasional use of fairy tales as easier to understand than my lapse into scientific explanations. For instance, as you acquire the ability to help heal yourself and others, you will be introduced to such scientific words as *psychoneuroimmunology* and *cyberphysiology* as indicators of the power of the mind to heal the body. Doesn't the concept of waving a magic wand sit better?

Scientists are now beyond the smallest particles of the atom in their investigation of matter and are penetrating into microscopic realms that are the frontiers of "the other side." They are beginning to see intelligence in the form of fields of energy filling all of space. As this energy manifests in the form of life, money, and love— as well as lakes, mountains, and prairies—we call this energy *creation*.

Creation is still going on in the universe. We are interested in its ability to do things on Earth. But what we used to believe in the centuries since Newton we no longer believe since the time of Einstein.

Here are some exciting developments in the form of new paradigms in the scientific belief system. First you will see the old Newtonian paradigm and then the new Einsteinian paradigm that has replaced it.

Old   The material world is made up of particles
      of matter separated in space and time.

New   The world is made up of interconnected
      energy fields that include space and time.

Old	The mind originates in the brain with intelligence in the nervous system and other parts of the body.
New	The mind fills the cosmos and beyond. It is part of a universal intelligence.
Old	The laws of nature are absolute and cannot be changed.
New	The human mind can trigger changes in natural law as we are its creators.
Old	We are human beings trying to be spiritual.
New	We are spiritual beings trying to be human.

End of lesson in quantum physics.

YOU ARE BEING CONTROLLED YET YOU ARE IN CONTROL

As I sit down to write this book, I have no idea how I am going to approach the subject. As I begin to write, thoughts come to me. I consider them to be my thoughts. But do I have a right to claim them as my own?

Some of them surprise me. How can they be mine if they surprise me? Am I receiving help? The answer is yes.

Let me explain this help to you scientifically. I relax when I sit down to write. I might even close my eyes to daydream about the next paragraph. Closing one's eyes relaxes the body. Daydreaming relaxes the mind. With the relaxed mind holding imaginative thoughts, brain waves are slowed and the right hemisphere is activated.

The right hemisphere connects one's intelligence to the universal intelligence just mentioned in the second new paradigm. It is in the creative realm, so the ideas are novel and creative.

Is that clear? Or would you prefer me to say "I have a good fairy"?

Does that mean that the good fairy is controlling me? Yes and no.

Yes, I am controlled because the ideas that come to me when I relax and daydream are not of my choosing. They are chosen for me and fed to me.

No, I am not controlled because I have sat at my desk, pen in hand, at my own choosing; I have chosen to write on this subject at this time. I have closed my own eyes and opened my own mind to such ideas purposefully.

Similarly, when you contact your good fairy, as you will later in this chapter, you will be in control of the process from beginning to end. But the delightful results that you will receive will be out of your control.

Can this be accurately described as similar to winning a lottery, or getting an unexpected tax refund, or receiving a sizable bequest from a deceased rich uncle? Or none of the above?

Of course, none of the above. "I must have a good fairy" is the reply you might prefer. As I do.

I am being controlled in writing this book. You are being controlled in reading it. My writing has an overall goal of my choice, but the ideas that flow to me are unique and original to me, obviously from a "source."

Similarly, you may underline parts while you read, or fold down pages that are important to you. Here is where you could be controlled by the same metaphysical force that put it into your hands in the first place.

I am going to give you an important step to take before you go one paragraph further.

Close your eyes, turn them slightly upward, and feel love and gratitude for whatever force caused you to have the book in your hands. Then ask for benefits.

You cannot read with your eyes closed. So put the book down now. Close your eyes, feel love, express gratitude, and ask for benefits.

Martin examined the newly unveiled car models. There was one that appealed to him and to his wife. But they had to have it in a certain color and Martin required an attachment that would enable him to tow his boat.

"We'll have to order it and it may take weeks," said the salesman.

"Order it," replied Martin.

Martin had already been working with his fairy godmother, doing services for people beyond the call of his investment business and finding unexpected good things happening to him. Later that week, he received a phone call from the car salesman.

"Better come right over."

When Martin arrived, there was the exact model of the car he ordered, in the precise color he and his wife preferred. What's more, it had the special boat towing attachment!

Fairy godmothers, genies, and other mythical magicians always reserve the right to refuse your request if they deem it unreasonable for one reason or another.

Remember the account of the little girl who was overheard by her parents praying before Christmas? She asked Santa Claus for twelve dolls. Of course, they bought her only one doll. On Christmas, when she had opened all her presents and found only one doll, she looked forlorn.

"What's the matter, dear?" asked her mother. "Did Santa Claus forget to bring you something you asked for?"

"He didn't forget," replied the child. "He just said no."

HOW TO ENSURE A YES FROM THE OTHER SIDE EVERY TIME

Even though we have not given you the simple procedure to contact your good fairy yet, it is not too early to talk about ensuring a "yes" for every request you make. Why not build up a sizable metaphysical bank balance starting now? Here is how.

Start monitoring your thoughts and feelings. Those that are down, dismal, and dark are negative thoughts. They are like a withdrawal from your metaphysical bank balance.

Those that are up, joyous, and loving are like deposits into your metaphysical bank account.

Since our actions follow our thoughts, you will find yourself living a better life when your thoughts are positive. Each day will be more productive and filled with beneficent and creative acts on your part.

Then watch that metaphysical bank balance zoom!

All the great teachers down through history have taught their followers how to live a better life. They were all on to the secrets of the other side.

Buddha taught non-attachment as a means of reducing greed and frustration. Moses taught rules for proper living. Lao-tzu taught how to live in harmony. Christ taught forgiveness. He also advocated going to what he called "the Kingdom within," which we can only surmise was the meditative state where "when you function within God's righteousness, all else will be added unto you."

Our world is far from perfect. Just as animals are combative, not only by reason of their place in the food cycle but also by dint of the "territorial imperative" that drives them to protect what they have and to acquire more, humankind is similarly driven. People are driven to have the most attractive mate, the most spacious home, the fanciest car. Business people struggle to expand their markets. Farmers struggle to expand their crop acreage. Politicians struggle to expand the numbers of their supporters.

Even the various religions have their own territorial imperatives as they struggle for more and more adherents. In fact, such struggles often have led to war.

The founders have not been understood, and certainly not followed. Instead, religions have been built largely around their lives rather than around their teachings.

They all taught there is a creative realm that we now call "the other side" and they all knew a basic fact about it that is still largely a secret to the rest of us. Here is that basic fact.

THE OTHER SIDE IS REALLY ON OUR SIDE

The other side came first. It is the source of the world. Creation is the ongoing goal and activity of the other side. It is taking place throughout the universe and under our noses as well.

This planet is changing daily as a result of creation. Land masses are moving toward and away from each other. Mountains are eroding and producing more flatlands. New islands are arising in the ocean.

You and I are helping with this process. We may not be moving mountains, but we are creating cities. We are inventing ways to improve the quality of life.

New experiences are heightening our awareness and expanding our consciousness. Interpersonal relationships, once harsh and cold, are becoming more loving and warm.

All this is creation, too. It is helping to perfect the Creator's handiwork. We are co-creators. We and the Creator are in the same boat. The Creator is on our side.

No wonder there are angels to help us, genies to manifest our needs, and fairies to grant our wishes.

Recently several network television shows have featured the work of angels in assisting individuals. In the process of saving lives, they often affect photographic film and leave ephemeral proof of their presence.

But if you insist on this kind of visible physical proof, you are missing the best part. You are better off being interested in the invisible part. Think about the security or support you can enjoy by being in touch with the other side.

In fact, from what you have learned about the other side so far in this chapter, whom do you pity the most:

a) A person with no visible means of support.

b) A person with no invisible means of support.

Of course, it's the latter individual who needs help most critically.

THE DOORWAY TO THE INVISIBLE WORLD

Is there a visible doorway to the invisible world?

To answer that, I ask you to close your eyes and imagine a doorway. Put the book down and do it now.

The doorway you just imagined is the doorway to the invisible world. I will soon be telling you how to open that doorway and, through it, contact the other side.

That's not a real doorway, you might think. "I just imagined it." Well, you've been listening to your parents and teachers who have been insisting that "it's just your imagination" and therefore, it's garbage. Don't blame them. They were taught that by their parents and teachers, who in turn were taught that by their parents and teachers, back, back, back, for generations.

The imagination is the forerunner of created reality. Better start teaching that to your children. Better yet, start demonstrating that to them.

Don't feel guilty that you are having trouble with this imagined doorway concept. If it came easily to everyone, this would be a much better world than it is. The reason is that you would be in touch with where you came from. You would have the guidance of the Creator and a host of helpers on an ongoing basis. As it is, you are in touch by verbal prayer, by knocking on wood, by throwing salt over your shoulders, or by crossing your fingers. These methods do not always work, though they would indeed always work *if you imagined them working.*

Suppose you were a human soul in the invisible world looking for a doorway to the visible world of material human bodies. Your doorway would be an embryo as it emerged from the womb. On the other hand, if you were a good fairy in the invisible world trying to do your job of helping somebody in the physical, visible world who was in need, it would be a lot easier to get there. You would create your own doorway by . . . . Sorry, I'm not a good fairy and I am at a loss as to how they do it. But they do it.

They do it when you use your doorway to the invisible world by imagining it, and . . . .

HOW TO OPEN THE DOORWAY TO THE INVISIBLE WORLD

What follows the "and" is essential: And, desiring help, you believe it is on the way and expect that desire will suffice.

Imagining a doorway is a static act. It just stands there. Closed. You need to imagine it opening, visualize help coming, and see your needs being met. All that is far from static. It is dynamic. It is action.

I will be giving you instructions throughout this book for using your imagination dynamically to get help from guardian angels and good fairies. I call these instructions Action Plans.

Each Action Plan will not only open the doorway to obtaining help for you but it will bring that help through the doorway and into your life.

Walter needed three thousand dollars to pay back mortgage payments or he risked losing his house. With a wife and three elementary school children, such a loss was unthinkable. I recommended an Action Plan to help him. When he read it, Walter agreed that the Action Plan seemed to fit his financial problem, and he put the instructions down and followed them. In about two minutes, he had completed it. He opened his eyes. No, no genie stood in front of him with three thousand dollars. The room was the same. In fact, for two weeks nothing at all happened except his time to pay the mortgage arrears was running out.

At the end of those two weeks, his wife decided to clean the attic. It was piled with old boxes, memorabilia, and endless photo albums left by her parents. As she thumbed through the albums, curious as to who were in the photos, she came across an album not with photos but with postage stamps. Apparently one of her parents had been a stamp collector. Neither she nor her husband was interested in acquiring this hobby, so they took the album to a professional philatelist in order to cash in on what little the stamp collection might be worth. They left with three thousand five hundred dollars!

Was it a miracle that saved their house? Or a good fairy?

WHAT YOU CAN BUILD FOR YOURSELF USING ACTION PLANS

The Action Plans provided on these pages are in strategic order. Each one builds on the ones before it.

If you skip around, you risk spinning your wheels. You may get nowhere. But by doing them in the order provided, each one takes you a step further on your path to expanding your power as a metaphysician, with magical forces at your beck and call.

Many scientists are taking a look at metaphysics today because their research has opened up new understanding of it. Quantum physics shows the never-before-accepted existence of "action at a distance." Their own consciousness and beliefs affect the outcome of their experiments in ways that belie their strongest conviction, namely that scientists are impartial observers.

Time and time again, they see how their own beliefs move the experiments in that direction. I could see this happening a half century ago. I was at the Massachusetts Institute of Technology at a time when the debate was raging whether light was wave or particle.

The standard test was passing light through an orifice. If it was a wave, it would break into smaller waves on the other side. If it was a particle, it would pile up in triangular form on the other side, with the peak directly opposite the orifice.

For scientists who imagined the outcome would be waves, light broke up into smaller waves. For scientists who imagined the outcome would be particles, light broke up in the triangular particle pattern.

Were the scientists controlling the outcome inadvertently by the creative power of their consciousness?

The late healer Olga Worrell was a more recent and dramatic example of how scientists affect the outcome of their experiments with their own minds. She was having her powers tested at what was then the Stanford Research Institute (SRI) when she stunned her hosts by affecting a cloud chamber. This measures cosmic rays entering the atmosphere by a shower of sparks. She was able to create a shower of sparks in the chamber on command.

"Can you do this at a distance?" asked one of the scientists.

"I'm going home now," she replied. "Phone me tomorrow evening."

Olga lived seven hundred miles away. They did not mean that great a distance, but they agreed. When they called her, she said, "Say when."

"Now, Olga."

Woosh, there was a shower of sparks in the cloud chamber. She repeated this twice on cue.

"Olga, we'd like to have a couple of our colleagues view this. Can we phone you the same time tomorrow?"

She agreed. The next night, with two skeptical scientists reluctantly standing by, they gave Olga the signal, "Now, Olga." Then again, "Now, Olga."

"I'm doing it," she assured them. But nothing was happening inside the cloud chamber. The two skeptics looked at each other as if to say "Rubbish" and left.

After they were gone, Olga was able to again affect the cloud chamber.

The consciousness of the two skeptics, who did not think it could be done, was just as much a part of the experiment as Olga herself. Two against. One for. The nays have it.

As you program yourself with Action Plans, you change your life. Your consciousness becomes pregnant with new benefits, unexpected blessings and fortunate events.

You begin to fulfill your role as a co-creator.

Here in general terms is what the usual Action Plan directs you to do:

- Relax and daydream.
- Imagine a doorway into the non-physical world.
- Mentally open the doorway and walk in.
- State your problem.
- Ask for a solution.
- Walk back out, leaving the doorway open.
- End your daydream, expecting the arrival of the solution.

Again, this is a general description of what you will be doing. Expect techniques to be added to make the actions more effective and the glorious results more immediate. Expect also that additional steps may be added that are uniquely suited to solving your more complicated problems.

In all Action Plans, you will begin by going through the "Main Steps For Relaxation" listed on page 19. You will augment these main steps with any of the optional ways to deepen relaxation listed beneath them in italics.

Also, in all Action Plans, you will follow your relaxation with the "Main Steps For Controlled Daydreaming" on page 20. You should seriously consider augmenting these main steps with the optional reinforcement steps listed below them in italics.

These main steps for relaxation, followed by the main steps for controlled daydreaming, will be indicated in the Action Plans to follow in this book merely with the instructions: 1. Relax. 2. Daydream. You will understand that these one-word instructions each cover the steps delineated on pages 19–21.

DAYDREAM TO ACTIVATE MYSTICAL POWERS

Your natural way to relax and your way of easily slipping into a daydreaming state is probably adequate to obtain the results you want. But *probably* is not definite enough and *adequate* is not thorough enough. So here are some techniques right from the start.

All of us are prone to daydreaming while waiting for some event. Perhaps you are waiting for the water to boil, or for your guests to arrive, or for your name to be called in a waiting room, or for the five o'clock news to be aired. These are okay for random daydreaming, but they are not the daydreaming times or places for your Action Plans.

To contact the invisible help you seek, Action Plans need to be done especially for that purpose and at a time and place unfettered by other more earthly matters.

Choose a time and place where you will not likely be interrupted or intruded on during the one to five minutes your Action Plan will require. A good time is when you rise in the morning or are about to retire at night. A good place is your bedroom. Any time that is private or any place where privacy is assured is the right time or place to sit comfortably, close your eyes, and begin to daydream.

Usually your daydreaming while driving or riding in a bus begins spontaneously. Minutes later, you realize you were daydreaming and often you check whether you made the correct turn or whether you passed your bus stop. You realize that you were turning over in your mind a trip you hoped to take, a meeting with another person that you fantasized might take place, or your being recognized for some special accomplishment you hoped to achieve.

This is natural daydreaming. It is self-starting and self-directing. It is not the daydreaming that is required in an Action Plan. The daydreaming you will be doing to activate help from the other side is controlled daydreaming. You do the controlling. You control your daydreams in accordance with the directions in each Action Plan.

If you are wondering why daydreaming can bring you health, money, love, and luck now, when it has never done this for you before, you are beginning to get the message. *Control* is an element that was missing in your daydreams up until now. Another missing element up until now: *Purpose.* Your daydreaming while waiting for the bus to come is merely to pass the time of day; your daydreaming while the teacher is at the chalkboard is to prevent boredom; your daydreaming while relaxing in your living room is to rest your mind.

Controlled daydreaming is a whole new ball of wax. It is about to revolutionize your life.

RELAX FOR MORE EFFECTIVE CONTROLLED DAYDREAMING

In a way, you will also control your relaxing. One cannot use the expression "controlled relaxation" because the word *control* involves a concept that is just the opposite of *relaxation.* Perhaps it is best to refer to a method for relaxing rather than the control of relaxation.

For centuries there have been techniques to heal the body. These mind therapies most always involve relaxation, either mental or physical or both, as part of their procedures. Some modern mind therapies that involve relaxation are biofeedback, the Alexander Technique, hypnosis, autogenic training, the Simonton Method, and the Feldenkrais Method, to name just a few.

The main reason that deep relaxation is a prerequisite for obtaining better mind-body communication is that relaxation slows the brain waves. When the brain waves are slowed, the right hemisphere of the brain—usually loafing on the job—gets active.

Read this paragraph twice: The right brain hemisphere is our connection to the creative realm. The creative realm is where all of the Creator's "staff" reside—angels, fairies, elves, genies, magicians.

When you relax, your mind is adjusted to a state where it can open the doorway to the invisible world.

How, then, do you relax? I have conducted hundreds of seminars all over the world, but I am not your best authority. A better authority is yourself. Suppose I list the main steps common to most methods of relaxation and then add a few optional steps you may want to add (these are in italics underneath the main steps).

Main Steps for Relaxation

1. Sit in a comfortable chair.

2. Close your eyes gently.

3. Take a few nice, deep breaths.

4. Check your body head to toe, relaxing tenseness.
   Count backwards from 20 to 1.
   Relax all the muscles, one by one, head to toe.

5. Feel heavier and heavier as you let go.
   Use affirmations such as "every time I relax
   this way, I go deeper, faster."

6. Visualize passive scenes that are relaxing.
   Select a place you have been where it was relaxing
   for you, and imagine you are there.

Review the main steps carefully. They comprise your method to relax in order to contact the help available to you—the standard approach to your fairy queen.

CONTROLLING YOUR DAYDREAMING

The instructions for relaxation that you have just read, plus the following instructions for controlled daydreaming, constitute the open sesame for the doorway to breathtaking help from the invisible world.

By following these steps, plus the special additional steps in each Action Plan, you are opening the combination lock for the doorway to Fairyland City.

It is like opening a safe packed with your life's treasures. This is because we now know that controlled daydreaming leads to the true reality. In fact, you are creating what you daydream in a controlled way.

I will now list the main controlled daydreaming steps to open the door to help from the invisible world, and include optional steps in italics beneath them for further ways to assure results.

Main Steps for Controlled Daydreaming

1. Mentally review the problem for which you seek help.
   Picture only briefly the details of the problem: emphasize a picture of the basic need (example: money).

2. Mentally affirm your belief in what you are doing and your expectation of results.
   After a number of sessions, pick one where you were successful all the way. Replay that.

3. Imagine a beautiful doorway, gate, or portal. Know it is the gateway that separates this physical world from its source—the creative realm.
   The more gilded, ornate, and jewel-encrusted, the better.

4. Feel love for the doorway and what lies beyond.
   The more genuinely you feel love, the more assured the response.

5. Bathe the beautiful doorway in brilliant white light.
   See the brilliant white light and use an imaginary rheostat to turn it up brighter still.

6. Move toward the doorway, knowing it will now open as you approach. It does.
   If it remains closed, you are feeling unworthy. You need to start over. This time, begin by relaxing and forgiving yourself.

7. Inside, imagine a fairyland of church steeples, towers, and mosques.
   Keep this fairyland scene in the background. The actions spelled out in the plan now should be done.

YOUR FIRST ACTION PLAN: HOW TO COME INTO EXTRA MONEY

This Action Plan manifests extra money for you quite speedily.

A woman found a $20 bill that same day.

A young man got an unexpected tax refund of $150 that same week.

A writer received a $5,000 assignment in three weeks.

A real estate woman, with no sale for months, made a $3,000 commission within three days.

Let me give you the details on the real estate woman. Margaret was moderately successful, but was experiencing a dry spell for nearly a year. A seller's market had turned into a buyer's market and now an influx of new real estate agents were competing for the thinner market.

Margaret was feeling low when she came to me for metaphysical assistance. I knew she would not be able to imagine the door to the creative realm opening, much less feel love and send light. So, I had to cheer her up and trigger a more optimistic mental climate before leading her through the Action Plan I am giving you now.

Three days after doing the Action Plan, she received a call from a man to whom she had shown a house ten weeks earlier, but who had decided to buy elsewhere.

"I'm back," he said. "If that house is still available, I'll take it at the asking price."

The sale meant a much-needed $3,000 commission to Margaret and a financial turn of events in her career.

Read these instructions over a couple of times until they become familiar to you. A friend or relative who is of like mind with you may read the step-by-step procedure to you as you do it, but it is better if you proceed alone.

Prepare your mental state. Wash away all feelings of financial limitation. Prepare yourself mentally to accept unlimited abundance. Practice relaxing according to the steps provided earlier on page 19. Also practice day-dreaming using the steps on pages 20–21. Once you are comfortable with the procedures for relaxing and using your imagination, follow the steps in this Action Plan if you are in need of some extra money.

Action Plan
for Extra Money

1. Relax.
2. Daydream.
3. Mentally open the doorway and walk in.
4. State firmly that you need more money.
5. Ask for help.
6. Place on your lap a dollar bill or higher denomination that you have collected in preparation for this Action Plan.
7. With your eyes still closed, visualize a ball of light about a foot over your head. Turn up the brilliance of the light. Permit the ball of brilliant light to slowly descend into your head, sinking slowly down your body until it reaches the level of your solar plexus (just above the navel). Now shine a beam of light out your navel and onto the money. See the money become aglow with energy. Turn off the beam. Imagine the money going out and away. Wait a moment. Now see a shower of money returning. See the air filled with countless returning bills. Slowly return the ball of light up your body and out of your head to the point above your head where it started. Dim the light of the ball. Imagine you are walking out the doorway and back to your chair; leave the door open. Open your eyes.
8. Spend the bill or change it within twenty-four hours.

WHY THE RICH GET RICHER
AND THE POOR GET POORER

Money is the symbol of abundance. The flow of money into and out of people's lives is probably, next to love, their greatest concern. This concern yields a strange situation: The rich get richer and the poor get poorer. This was recognized even as far back as the writing of the Bible.

Can you understand this apparent unfairness now? A poor man daydreams about his lack and pictures a difficult tomorrow. Since daydreams are creative, the poor man's worrisome daydreams are perpetuating his lack. Meanwhile, the rich man is having different daydreams. He is counting his money and imagining all the things he will be doing with his growing wealth. So the rich man is perpetuating and increasing his abundance through creative daydreaming.

The energy of consciousness is real energy. It is called psychotronic energy. When you relax and daydream, you focus your psychotronic energy on the subject of your mental images. This is creative energy.

So you tend to create what you picture mentally.

Start now to eliminate worry, pessimism, and other negativity from your relaxed thoughts. You are getting in your own way.

Instead, start making mental friends with the powers that be in the invisible world. Do this in any way that comes to you. They thrive on your expectation and belief, your love and recognition.

And when they thrive, you thrive.

2

HOW TO LOSE YOUR UGLY BEAST DISGUISE AND MANIFEST THE AMAZING HERO INSIDE

Remember the fairy tale *Beauty and the Beast* still being frequently told in books and on screen? Beauty meets the ugly Beast when she wanders into his castle. He falls in love with her and, when releasing her to her freedom, says he will die if she does not return. Back home, she remembers her promise to return. When she does, she finds the Beast dying.

"Don't look at me," he whispers, turning his head away. "I am so ugly."

"Please don't die," says Beauty, taking one of his paws in her hand. "I love you." Her tears fall onto his coarse fur.

When she opens her eyes, gone are the claws and fur of a beast. Instead, she holds the hands of a handsome young man.

"A wicked fairy used her evil magic on me long ago," he explains. "She changed me from a royal prince to an ugly beast. The spell could only be broken if a kind and honest girl came freely to love me."

Beauty and her prince are married the very next week, and they live happily ever after.

If you think about the moral of the story, it is easy to see that kindness and honesty are qualities that have a spiritual strength, while love can work miracles.

Kindness, honesty, and love. These attributes can open the doorway to the invisible world of miraculous events.

The Action Plans on these pages are powerful applications of the ability of the mind to reach back to where it came from, and to where its roots still remain, in order to cause changes in the physical world. As powerful as these applications are, they will not work to do harm, to create problems, to curse, or to control others against their will.

They will work—and work well—to assist those who are kind, honest, and loving.

HAVE WE CONFUSED THE REAL AND THE UNREAL?

Bedtime stories, fairy tales, and myths are ways to trigger the mind to take a giant step into reality.

Yes, you read that correctly. The real world is the cause behind this physical world. It is the creative realm. It is the true reality. It is indeed a giant step into this creative, causal realm. When we arrive there, we have no concrete words to describe it. We can talk about it only in terms of feelings and fairies.

This world of skyscrapers, jet planes, boiled lobsters, and politics is unreal. It is all phenomenal. The materials that comprise it are themselves comprised of atoms, which are in turn pure energy.

So, the chair you are sitting in appears to be solid, but it is energy in space. The color you see on the wall opposite you, perhaps light blue, is not the true reality. It is everything except blue. It looks blue because it accepts all light wavelengths except the wavelength of the color blue. It rejects blue and so the blue comes back and you see the wall as blue. In reality, it is not blue and it is not as solid as it appears to you to be.

Other ways to trigger the mind to take a giant step into the causal, creative realm is to sit by a babbling brook and daydream or enjoy a beautiful sunset and contemplate. You might then get a glimpse of reality. You could discuss it with your mate or your best friend but despite your use of words with deepest meanings, you could not adequately or fully do justice to your experience.

There are no perfect words for the heavenly perceptions we are fortunate to glory in momentarily. When we try to describe it, the moment is changed to fit the words; fleeting as it is, the magic moment is totally destroyed by the words. We return to the hot and cold, hard and soft, pleasant and unpleasant apparent realities of this physical world.

We are hypnotized by it. The deeper we get into its failures and its successes, the further we get from the steeples, spires, and mosques of the imaginary world behind the magic doorway.

HOW TO REINFORCE THE REALITY OF THE DAYDREAM WORLD

The Aborigines in Australia remember that their ancestors had a way of meditating called Dreamtime. Tales of Dreamtime have survived to this day.

Many bear a striking resemblance to stories in the Bible as well as the religions or folklore of other cultures and lands. For instance, the Ancestor, the Creator, spoke to the Aborigines from the trunk of a great tree, exhorting them to return to the path of righteousness. This is similar to Jehovah, the Creator, speaking to Moses out of a burning bush and calling for him to help his people back to the laws of righteousness.

Dreamtime for the Aborigines was a time for putting the visible world aside and tuning in to the invisible world that created it. There they found ways to achieve their goals by some mysterious force of cunning, fortitude, and fortune.

Controlled daydreaming by you and me, thousands of years later, can produce the same good luck. We can tap the forces of creation—call them witches, fairies, genies, magicians, handsome princes, or even God—and produce a sudden crystallization of energy into matter that adds up to an unexplainable bonanza.

You can reinforce the reality of the daydream world for you by acts of kindness, honesty, and love.

You can reinforce the reality of the daydream world through desire, expectation, and belief.

You can reinforce the reality of the daydream world by daydreaming how you can make this a better world to live in and by following through with what comes to you to do.

THE MORE REAL THE DAYDREAM WORLD IS TO YOU, THE MORE REAL ITS GIFTS BECOME

There is a tribe of native people living at the summit of the Colombian Mountains in South America. They retreated there centuries ago when the Spanish were conquering the area. They allow no visitors and have few advantages of the civilized world. They are called the Mamas.

As civilization has moved closer and closer, its ravages of the natural environment has made dramatic changes to the Mamas' habitat. For this reason, they allowed television cameras and interviewers in so that their warning to "younger brother" might be widely heard. The warning: Respect nature and its laws.

One highlight of the interviews was the revelation that occasionally they require a mother to give birth far into a dark cave. The infant is reared in that cave and never exposed to the outside world until eight to ten years of age.

The child that emerges from the cave is different than all of the other children. Not having been hypnotized by the physical world, the child has remained rooted in the non-physical world. He or she is still connected to the Creator. As a result, that child knows all wisdom: "That bush heals the stomach." "That leaf heals the heart." "That plant stops pain."

The child is not only a natural healer, but has unerring instinct, impressive guessing ability, and the gift of prophecy.

By insulating the growing infant from the material world life, the Mamas are able to create a genius. That is because the growing infant has been protected against the programming of limitation to which all growing humans are subjected: limited health, limited life expectancy, limited wealth, limited intelligence, and limited love.

We can all reprogram ourselves. We can all begin to restore our original programming of no limitation. We can all align our physical and spiritual worlds.

That is the purpose of the next two Action Plans. The first will move you to that joining of consciousness. The second will give you official membership in the Halls of Plenty.

HOW TO DREAM THE IMPOSSIBLE
DREAM AND MAKE IT POSSIBLE

If your consciousness were married to the consciousness that fills the unseen world, and if your consciousness of limitation was re-taught that this is a world of infinite plenty—be it money, travel, or love—the result would be an invincible you, capable of attaining your every wish.

If you suspect that you may be part of the great universal consciousness that fills all space, that is not enough. Take the late Walter Russell. As a leading physicist, he was the co-discoverer of heavy water, which introduced the atomic age. He was a registered architect, with buildings in Manhattan. He was the sculptor of three presidents. He was also a poet, author, philosopher, composer, and teacher. His biographer called him "the man who tapped the secrets of the universe."

During his final years, he lived with his wife in a castle atop the Shenandoah Mountains of Virginia. I visited them there and viewed his accomplishments.

"You must have a tremendous amount of faith, Walter," I commented later over tea.

"I have no faith at all," he countered. "I know."

You, too, must have more than trust or faith. You must know that you are part of this universal consciousness. You must know that it not only fills this visible universe, but the invisible causal realm as well. So, resolve now to go beyond "I'll take your word for it for the time being" or "What have I got to lose?"

Instead, anticipate this next Action Plan with an understanding of its potential impact. Expect it to enlarge your very being. Know it has the capability of making possible even your most "impossible" dream.

A TWO-MINUTE MENTAL TRIP THAT MULTIPLIES YOUR METAPHYSICAL POWER

To ready yourself for this powerful Action Plan, sit for a while and contemplate this concept: nobody is sitting in the chair with you. Your body is apparently separate. And because your head, which contains your brain, is a closed compartment, your consciousness is separate.

Now, remind yourself that your body is energy: every atom of your body can be transformed into energy. So, your brain is not enclosed in your consciousness, is not a prisoner of your skull. Your consciousness is expandable.

When you have thought about this scientific understanding of your body and your consciousness, you are ready to begin.

ACTION PLAN

to Expand Consciousness

1. Relax.
2. Daydream.
3. Mentally open the doorway, but do not enter.
4. Envision a sphere of light around you. You are bathed in this light. It is the energy of your consciousness.
5. Imagine this sphere of light expanding in all directions. It spreads over the town you live in, the state, the whole country. It also expands beyond the doorway and lights up the invisible world—its towers, mosques, and steeples.
6. Your light of consciousness envelops planet Earth. Send your light out to encompass our entire solar system. As it joins with the light of our sun, it is joining with universal consciousness.
7. Send out your light of consciousness to encompass other suns in our galaxy, then out to other galaxies. Feel at one with universal consciousness.
8. Now bring your consciousness back to this galaxy, this solar system, this planet, this town, this spot.
9. State mentally: "My consciousness is one with universal consciousness. Universal life energy surges through me as I go forth."
10. Leaving your sphere of light around you and the doorway still open and bathed in it, end your Action Plan by opening your eyes.

With your Action Plan ended, do you feel your body and mind as separate as you did a few minutes ago? There is a difference. The fact is, you are no longer as separate in your consciousness as you conceived yourself to be before because you have rejoined your consciousness with a larger consciousness.

Since this larger consciousness is the creative consciousness, you will have more of the creative consciousness as part of your normal life, so it will not be normal anymore. Your days will be on a higher level. You will be more loving, more understanding, more aware, more enlightened. It is as if you have graduated to a higher level of existence.

If I could, I would hand you a diploma.

HOW TO BEGIN A CHANGE FROM WEAK PATSY TO STRONG HERO

Many western myths and fairy tales contain a character called the dragon. Symbolically, the dragon stands for greed. In his cave are gold and virgins that he protects. When the dragon's threat to someone results in that someone's slaying the dragon, that someone becomes a hero.

The purpose of the tale is to show that the dragon is the ego of the hero, and by slaying the dragon, the hero has freed himself from the bonds of gross materialism and has entered a new life that contains both the known (present) and the unknown (future), the visible and the invisible.

I am not going to ask you to slay any fire and brimstone dragons, but when you invite a closer relationship with the invisible realm, you confront a dragon, whether you like it or not. You slay the dragon of gross materialism as an exclusive way of life together with all the conflict and stress that such a life entails.

Materialism is a weakness. The bank accounts, possessions, and investments certainly add up to one great visible means of support. It is a great support today, but bears no promise for tomorrow. The weakness of gross materialism lies in its impermanence.

Slay that dragon and you begin to enjoy the wisdom of material insecurity. It brings with it a freedom to know the unknown fearlessly—for a lifetime.

You do not lose your money or give away your possessions. They remain yours, but you release your dependency on them. Something else comes into view for you.

Remember the sight you saw through your imaginary doorway into the realm of magic? It was a fairyland scene of glittering spires, golden domes, and sparkling steeples.

Let me tell you what some of those buildings are. There is the Universal Bank. You've heard of a world bank. The Universal Bank has access to all the wealth in the universe.

There is also the Eternal Life Health Spa. Most health spas that you know cannot make such a dramatic promise. But this one can. It recognizes that you are energy. What did you learn about energy in high school? You learned that it cannot be created or destroyed, only changed from one form to another.

One of the domed buildings is the Universal Trade Center. Give something of value and you receive something of value. Instead of paying a commission for the transaction, you receive a bonus. Another spired building is the Supreme Court, where all wrongs are righted.

There are many more, but one of the grandest buildings, with countless spires and steeples, is the Universal House of Wisdom. There, one has immediate access to Infinite Intelligence. Stressful decisions, stressful relationships, and stressful problems are dissolved in magical solutions that dispel stress and create joy, peace, and love. In fact, here the love of the Creator for you is under such high atmospheric pressure that it permeates the heaviest clothing and the toughest skin.

YOU BECOME A HERO WHEN YOU PAY YOUR MEMBERSHIP FEE TO FAIRYLAND CITY

Would you like to have a lifetime pass to this Fairyland City that entitles you to use the Universal Bank whenever you need more money? The lifetime pass also gives you membership in the Eternal Life Health Spa and the Universal Trade Center. Free access to the Universal House of Wisdom can do so much for you that it's worth the price of admission to Fairyland City just by itself.

What is the price you must pay for a lifetime pass to Fairyland City? The bad news is that the price is pretty steep. The good news is that you have already started to pay it.

If you have done the exercises and Action Plans so far in Chapter 1 and this chapter, and if you do the second Action Plan spelled out a few pages ahead, you are almost there. There is just one more thing you have to do.

You must read one fairy tale.

I know this is an unreasonable thing to ask you to do, especially at your age. But it is an ironclad requirement. After all, how can you expect to receive the benefits that abound in Fairyland if you refuse to read a fairy tale at this meaningful moment?

Here's one that is short and to the point. It is important to get the point. Otherwise you might not be considered for membership. (I'll help you.)

A Fairy Tale

In a garden with two rosebushes, one white and one red, lived two sisters, Snow White and Rose Red. They lived in a red and white cottage with their widowed mother. They were loving to each other, always diligent, and always cheerful. Snow White enjoyed staying at home and helping her mother with housework or reading aloud to her. Rose Red loved the outdoors—picking flowers, chasing butterflies, et cetera.

One bitterly cold, snowy evening, there came a knock at the door. Opening it, they saw a big shaggy bear. The girls were terrified, but the mother let him in to lie on the hearth as she realized he was a good, honest creature who would do them no harm. At daybreak, they let him out. From then on, he came each evening at the same hour. He'd let the girls play with him, too.

When spring came, the bear said, "I must leave now and go to the forest to protect my treasure from the wicked dwarfs. So long as the ground is frozen, they remain underground, but now with the thaw, they emerge to steal what they can." Off he went.

Gathering faggots in the woods sometime later, the girls came upon an old dwarf who had caught his long white beard in a cleft in a tree. Snow White, who always seemed prepared, pulled out her little scissors and snipped his beard to free him. He reached down under the tree's roots, pulled up a bag of gold, and went off shouting curses at the girls for spoiling his beautiful beard. A couple of times more, they rescued him, and each time he ran off with a bag of gold or jewels that had lain hidden in the ground.

The last time, as he was about to run off cursing them, the bear trotted up. Terrified, the dwarf offered to give back all that he had stolen, begging the bear to turn on the girls. But the bear, paying no attention, pounced on the dwarf, killing him. As he did so, his bear pelt fell from him, revealing a handsome prince. He told the girls that the dwarf had placed him under a spell but now, at last, he was freed of the curse by the dwarf's demise.

The prince married Snow White. His younger brother, also a prince, married Rose Red. They lived happily ever after. The End.

Please think about this tale and then state its lesson.

I'll give you some hints. Note how good Rose Red and Snow White are. This is brought out in the first few lines. Notice how the mother intuitively knows that the bear means no harm. The old dwarf cares only for his body and his possessions; he is obviously the epitome of how we ourselves should not live our lives. And what does he lose in the end? He goes back into the ground where he really had chosen to be.

Do you see yourself as the bear (a person with helpful intentions) or the dwarf (a person with selfish self-interest)?

RELAXING AND SEEING
IS THE KEY TO BEING

I know a person who is always worrying and imagining the worst. We were walking across a park in Hawaii when I saw her looking around nervously.

"What are you worrying about?" I asked.

"Snakes," she replied.

"Worrying wastes your creative energy," I reminded her. "Anyway, we don't have any snakes in Hawaii."

"See," she exclaimed triumphantly, "worrying works!"

When you relax and visualize, you are programming your great mental computer to create what you are picturing.

Do you want a better job? Relax and picture yourself in a better job.

Do you want to be more affluent or wealthy, with a better car or house, or travel more? Relax and picture yourself that way.

Do you want to weigh less, or be a non-smoker, or drink less? Relax and see yourself that way.

Do you want to be a better bowler? Relax and see yourself making strike after strike. Or a better tennis player, or golfer, or able to run a tractor better?

Here are some simple rules to follow that make your relaxation and picturing sessions work faster and better for you.

- Hold these relaxation sessions two or three times a day.
- Choose a place that is quiet and where you won't be disturbed.

- Relax deeply. You can deepen your relaxation by counting from five to one, additional times if necessary, or by occasionally taking another deep breath.

- You can deepen your relaxation even more by imagining peaceful places.

- Before picturing yourself reaching your goal, see yourself as you are now so as to identify the problem.

- When picturing yourself as you would like to be, add light to the picture, as if you were turning on the lights, or turning up a rheostat. This adds energy.

- When you end your relaxing and picturing session, tell yourself that you will feel wide awake and great. Then, when you open your eyes, know that you feel good because you are on the way to reaching your goal.

Have you some goal you would like to reach? Decide now what area you would like to work on. It could be a skill you wish to improve (typing, handiwork, cooking). It could be a habit you want to let go of (overeating, smoking, hair twirling, nail biting, excessive drinking). It could be a personal condition you want to end (nervousness, worry, fear). It could be a goal you want to attain (popularity, wealth, a mate).

We all have more than one desire. Decide on a priority. You will work on that first. Later, you can work on the next desire or goal.

Do you mind if I make a suggestion for a priority that you might like to consider?

The very fact that you have not reached a number of goals in your life to date might indicate that you do not consider yourself worthy enough. You might not have enough self-esteem.

Here are some mental pictures that will build up your self-esteem.

- See yourself as the star of a parade.

- Picture yourself being carried on the shoulders of your teammates, hero of the game.

- See yourself on the dais at a banquet. Speakers are praising you. It is a testimonial dinner to you.

- There is an office. On the door is the word "President." When you open the door and look in, you see yourself sitting behind a huge desk.

- A huge crowd is milling around outside a theater. The marquee sign has your name in lights.

Get the picture? Any pictures of yourself that have you as a star serve to move you in the direction of actually being a star. Put a light around these mental pictures. Give them more creative energy.

This is not big enough to be an Action Plan, but it is important to you. So . . . .

An Exercise for Self-Esteem

1. Relax.
2. Picture how you want to be.
3. Hold a few such pictures of yourself, the hero, in your mind for a few seconds each.
4. End by affirming yourself to be wide awake and feeling more capable than before.

Now you are ready to do goal-reaching exercises. Pick a priority. Relax. See yourself as you are now, without the skill you desire. Change the picture to visualize your skillful doing of the desired activity, surrounded by light. End by opening your eyes, feeling wide awake and more capable than before.

Remember always that relaxing and seeing yourself the way you want to be—younger, more agile, healthy, having a skill, reaching a goal—is the key to being what you are seeing. You become more perfect.

It takes only one or two minutes but moves you months, even years, ahead.

YOU NOW GET THE KEYS TO FAIRYLAND CITY

You have grown in the past two chapters. The eyes of the other side are on you. They see you as a more effective co-creator and are willing to help you.

What this amounts to is that the keys to Fairyland City are now available to you for the asking.

Would you like your own key to the Universal Bank? Subsequent chapters will give you Action Plans that enable you to use the key to enter the bank, approach a teller, and cash a check for whatever you need.

Would you like a lifetime membership pass to the Eternal Life Health Spa, enabling you to keep yourself healthy, youthful, and energetic? There you can swim in a heated pool, sit in a sauna, partake of a 1,000-foot salad bar, and do aerobics effortlessly. The Spa offers a place for you to help heal yourself and others.

Would you like to be able to enter the Universal House of Wisdom any time you have a problem, to sit in one of its meditation rooms to contact Universal Intelligence for answers, ideas, and solutions? Here is your source of creativity, inspiration, and invention.

Presumably, you have been saying yes, yes, yes. You would be crazy not to want the key to this city. But I would be crazy to give it to you just like that. I would stand to lose my key. The reason is that care must be taken in screening all applicants.

Intelligent people are often able to scan a book in an hour or less and gain some insight into its scope and content. However, the person who is not yet a metaphysician can never become a metaphysician by merely flipping the pages or even reading slowly.

To become a metaphysician—that is, to be eligible for a key to Fairyland City and all of its magic—you must experience the following:

- Relaxation of the body
- Relaxation of the mind
- Imaging mental pictures
- Visualizing a doorway to the invisible world
- Controlled daydreaming
- Using affirmations
- Visualizing brilliant white light
- Expanding your consciousness
- Feeling love for the universe
- All the Action Plans and exercises so far

This means you have followed all of the directions so far in this book. If so, you are ready for the Action Plan in which you receive the key to Fairyland City, enabling you to use its financial, health, and problem-solving resources.

Begin by resting in a chair and reviewing in your mind the immensity of what is about to take place.

When you have thought about the grandiose power of the invisible world and how it will be made available to you through the facilities of Fairyland City, you are ready to begin. Read the entire Action Plan before doing it.

You may need to read this several times in order to lead yourself through it with your eyes closed. It is recommended that, rather than opening your eyes to check the next step, you ask an understanding friend or relative to read it to you.

ACTION PLAN

to Get the Key for Fairyland City

1. Relax.
2. Daydream.
3. With the doorway enveloped in your bright white light, mentally open it.
4. Imagine you are walking through the door. As you look ahead, the first thing you see is a beautiful garden. There are rose bushes in full bloom. Note the differently colored roses. Now walk up to a rose bush and look closely at one of the blossoms. There is a drop of water from a recent shower glistening in the light. Can you see all the colors of the rain now reflected in that one drop of water? There, you now have the key to Fairyland City.
5. As your guide, just this first time, I will lead you to the main facilities. First, the Universal Bank. We are approaching its domed building. Notice the impressive columns at the entrance. We climb the marble steps and enter. See, it looks just like any bank: tables with checks to fill out, and cashiers waiting behind counters to help you. In this bank you are not concerned with your account balance. It is constantly replenished. All you require is need. It does not respond to checks made out to satisfy greed, but it responds quickly to checks made out to fulfill needs. Sometimes it pays in cash that materializes for you back in the material world, or it might deliver other ways that fill the need—again, back in the material world.

continued

6. Let's leave and visit that building nearby with the lotus blossom pool. It's the Eternal Life Health Spa. You can visit here anytime now that you know how. Just walking into this entrance hall with all the herbs and plants is a tonic to your health. Light seems to be emanating from the floor, walls, and ceiling. It is life energy. Sit in one of these Jacuzzis and you are rejuvenated. To the right are exercise rooms, to the left are massage rooms. If you have a serious condition, stand in front of that mirror over there. Fix up your image in the mirror, thus helping to fix up yourself in reality.

7. Next stop is the Universal House of Wisdom. It is the building with the tall steeple and smaller spires. It is always good for your soul to stop before entering this building and thank the Creator for your existence. As you enter, notice how everything is iridescent and a silent hush prevails. One whole side of this immense space— to your right—acts as a laboratory outfitted with all the tools and equipment that ever were, are, or will be. Your key allows you its use to fill any need. To the left are receiving benches. Meditate there and answers come.

8. There are other powerful places in Fairyland City. You can visit them later at will. Meanwhile, leave your key with one of the roses by admiring one on the way out.

9. At the doorway, repeat mentally, "My consciousness is one with universal consciousness. Universal life energy surges through me as I go forth."

10. Leaving the doorway open, pass through it and end by opening your eyes and affirming, "Wide awake!"

HOW TO TAP THE CREATIVE POWER
OF FAIRYLAND CITY

When you have a chance later today or tomorrow, sit and contemplate Fairyland City. Realize the immense support you have available to you in the invisible, creative realm epitomized by Fairyland City.

Review the unlimited resources awaiting your needs in the Universal Bank. You cannot list these resources on your financial statement, but you can draw on them as needed. Remember the Eternal Life Health Spa. Maybe some day your family can become members, too. And, the mightiest of powers are yours in the Universal House of Wisdom. No computer can compare.

Hopefully you have now advanced your belief system to the point where it will not deter you or hold you back. You will have a desire. You will believe that a visit to Fairyland City will help you. After your visit there, you will expect a beneficial result. And your expectations will be met.

Do not discuss Fairyland City with family, friends, or business colleagues who are not of like mind. They have all been educated to understand this effect of creation—the material world—but not creation itself. When you talk about the invisible realm, they cannot relate to it. Anything people cannot relate to is, for them, frightening, off the wall, or plain crazy. Their negative reactions will serve only to water down your own desire, belief, and expectancy.

Play it safe. Attribute it all to luck, at least for now. Lady Luck parcels out a lot of loot, and can come up with some amazing "coincidences" and "synchronicities."

Lady Luck can even lead you to the right answers or to the people who have the wherewithal and know-how to help you.

Oh, I forgot to tell you. Lady Luck lives in the castle just beyond the Universal House of Wisdom in Fairyland City.

3

THE SECRET TO EMERGING FROM THE DARK LABYRINTH OF NEED INTO THE BRIGHT LIGHT OF GOOD FORTUNE

This is a universe of abundance. It is also a universe of free will.

You and I have the freedom to feel limited. If you choose to feel limited, the universe bows to your will. You become limited.

You may still find yourself doing this limited trip with your consciousness despite the exercises and Action

Plans in the first two chapters. Don't feel guilty if this is so. It is not a product of your weakness. Rather it is the product of the hypnotizing power of the limited time and limited space in this material world.

The material world is working on our mind from morning to night. Take space. We wake up in a room. It is limited space. A box. We go to the bathroom. Again, limited space, a box. We eat breakfast in a box, ride to work in a box, and spend all of our working day in one or more boxes. When it's over, what do we put ourselves into? Another box.

And so it is that we build personal prisons for ourselves, prisons of limited money, limited ability, and limited love. Most of us live our entire lives in such self-made prisons. Then something happens. Some people find that the prison door was never locked, and now they can walk out, free of limitation, into a world of boundless joy, love, and health.

That "something" has already happened for you.

You are able to fill all needs and solve all problems because you have access to the limitless bounty of the universe. You are no longer confined to the limitations of the physical world. You are free.

Suppose you have suffered a severe financial setback. As a result, you are under stress, subject to headaches, suffering from loss of sleep, and totally without the glimmer of a solution as to how to proceed.

Coming up: One trip to Fairyland City.

PREPARING FOR A PROFITABLE TRIP TO FAIRYLAND CITY

When I myself am ready for a trip to Fairyland City, I prepare for it. Here are some of the things I do:

I relax and enjoy a few sessions of controlled daydreaming, using pictures of myself starring in various roles.

I look in on somebody who might need help, straightening things up, perhaps running an errand, certainly offering words of praise and encouragement.

I relax and send my consciousness aloft to embrace universal consciousness.

Then I am ready for my trip. I relax, daydream, open the doorway, and get my key inside the garden where that water drop on a rose reflects all the colors of the rainbow.

My first visit, if I was under stress, for example, would be to the Eternal Life Health Spa. There I would first have a gentle massage, take a fulfilling nap, and ask the laboratory for a headache preventative. They supply the water and I swallow it on the spot.

My next visit is to the Universal Bank. Sure enough, there is a supply of checks on the table. I figure out my needs and write on the check, "Pay to the order of Robert B. Stone, three thousand dollars!" I walk to a teller and he or she accepts it. I leave knowing the payment (in dollars or other assets) is on the way.

I am now ready to solve my business situation so that I don't ever fall into this abyss again. The Universal House of Wisdom is just a few controlled daydreaming steps away. I stand outside, looking up at its sparkling spires and radiant steeple. I stop, bow my head, and thank the Creator for the blessings of life, love, and laughter that I enjoy. I am now ready to enter.

Once inside, I turn left and sit on one of the meditation benches. In my controlled daydreaming, I review the depleted bank account. Business has been fairly good, but what should I be doing that I am not doing to get ahead instead of behind?

I attune my awareness to a more universal awareness. This is equivalent to being in tune with a universal intelligence. I feel love and closeness. I wait.

Suddenly, a picture enters my daydreams. It is of my bookkeeper. He is stuffing money into his wallet—my money. Simultaneously, the thought comes: "Your bookkeeper is falsifying the books and pocketing the profits."

On my way out of Fairyland City, I leave the key with one of the beautiful roses. At the doorway, I stop and affirm mentally, "My consciousness is one with universal consciousness. Universal life energy surges through me as I go forth." I open my eyes and mentally say, "Wide awake!"

I sit there stunned. I never suspected. Slowly events turn through my mind that convince me I need to do some of my own auditing. I get up and do it. In the process, my bookkeeper realizes I am on to something. Within one week, he confesses, apologizes, and makes restitution—three thousand dollars.

OTHER WAYS TO BENEFIT FROM FAIRYLAND CITY

Throughout the rest of these pages, there will be instructions on making a better life for yourself and for others using the creative power of Fairyland City.

Not everything is solved in Fairyland City. Some matters are so tied in with the material world that other methods are indicated. These other methods will also be provided on the pages ahead together with instructions as to when and how to use them.

I would like to give you a glimpse of how some people were helped by the creative power of Fairyland City.

Take Anna. She was bothered monthly by acute menstrual distress. She went to the Eternal Life Health Spa. In the laboratory there, she was able to instantly create a life-sized energy replica of her own body. Examining it, she could see the problem. Using appropriate tools, she corrected the problem in her energy body. Since the energy body forms the physical body, the correction she made in her energy body also took place in her physical body. Her menstrual problem was gone.

Wendy had a problem with her principal in the junior high school where she had taught for five years. He was making unwanted passes at her and had even pawed her several times when passing her on a stairway. Now she had been called into his office and her work in the classroom was criticized. There was clearly no reason for this and his intentions were obvious.

She went to Fairyland City, through the garden, and directly to the Universal House of Wisdom. One of the rooms there is identified by the single word "telephone."

Wendy walked into that room. She had been there before on another matter, so she knew that there was really no telephone there, but one could still make imaginary calls through controlled daydreaming.

These calls did not go through a telephone. They are more like broadcasting from person to person. This used to be called mental telepathy, but now it is called a more scientific term: subjective communication. It goes from your higher consciousness to the higher consciousness of the person you visualize. And you never get a wrong number.

The advantage over a telephone is that your words bypass the programmed mind of the lower self and appeal automatically to the higher self. Higher selves do not engage in sexual harassment. So, once Wendy completed her subjective conversation, her principal never again caused her a problem.

One more, before we move on. Larry was a mess. He was so shy that he was unable to talk to a member of the opposite sex, and even when he spoke to another male, he looked down, spoke in a monotone, and only said a few words at a time. He was working as a bag filler in a supermarket for two years with no prospect of a better job. Larry's father paid for a training course in relaxation, controlled daydreaming, and self-esteem.

After the course, Larry used trips to Fairyland City daily in order to visit the Universal Bank. There his withdrawals were not in dollars, but in self-worth. Soon he was such a live wire with checkout customers that they made him a department supervisor.

You will be given detailed instructions on the multitude of ways to avail yourself of the powers in Fairyland City as we proceed.

CLEANSING ACTIONS THAT IMPROVE YOUR RESULTS

There is no such animal as a perfect human being.

We are all polluted.

We are polluted by exposure to the civilized world, to our own thoughts, and to the thoughts imposed on us by society and the media.

This pollution acts as resistance. The more the pollution, the more the resistance to the flow of life energy. In fact, the more the pollution, the less successful the creative energy emanating from Fairyland City is able to work for us.

Fortunately, ancient cultures have recognized this and found ways to help purify our auras, or energy bodies, and to release physical tensions arising from mental stress.

I would be derelict in my duty to you if I did not at least present some of these purifying exercises to you, and recommend that you take time as soon as possible to do them all. There are four. You will need another person to help you. This companion will also benefit as you will.

Purifying Exercises

1. This is borrowed from Yoga. They call it the lion, and well they might. Sitting side by side with your companion, fling both arms out in front of you, open your eyes wide, and your mouth even wider. Straining forward with your arms, stick out your tongue as far as possible and try to touch your chin with it. Try harder. Now both of you turn and look at each other. . . . Sorry about that. I could not resist. It is not part of the offered yoga procedure—looking at each other—but you must admit, it adds fun to the exercise. The purpose of the exercise is to break up patterns embedded in the facial muscles resulting from repeated facial expressions. It also brings increased blood circulation to the released muscles, adding to a more youthful look.

2. This next exercise requires you to stand. It is the legacy of ancient Hawaiians. Their health leaders were known as Kahunas. These Kahunas were quite purified and knew how to keep themselves that way. By kicking their legs a few times, they visualized impurities leaving their bodies. And that's indeed what happened. After standing, walk a few steps away from where you were sitting, and kick the right leg three times, knowing that you are ridding yourself of unwanted energies. Now do the same with your left leg. You may now return to your seat. The reason I had you move away from your seat to do this is because it would not be appropriate for you to sit back down in your own garbage.

3. In this third exercise, you will sweep each other's energy fields. This, too, is borrowed from the Kahunas. To sweep an energy field, you hold both hands, palms down, to within a few inches from your partner's body. Starting at the head, sweep your hands down to the floor. As your partner slowly turns, continue this sweeping motion, using a flip of your hands when they near the floor. When your partner has turned a full 360 degrees, it is done. Fling your hands a few times to get rid of impurities. Now it is your turn.

4. This final exercise is done also in a standing position. Its origins are more modern and are from the approach called toning. Watch me as I demonstrate it for you. I raise my arms up above my head. I fling them down to the floor while letting out a horrible groan. The groan is horrible because it permits all the negativity within me to be expelled. I do this three times. The third time, I remain a moment in the arms-down position, then I raise my arms while toning a rising sound that indicates I am replacing the negative with exquisite positive. I reach for the ceiling with this exultant cry. I do this three times. You can both do this together. Ready? Go!

THE MOST ESSENTIAL CLEANSER IN ANYBODY'S LIFE

I said there were to be only four of these cleansing exercises. There is really a fifth. But I hesitate to call it an exercise. It is more than an exercise.

You would not call breathing in and out throughout the day an exercise. It would not be called an exercise to quench your thirst or eat three meals a day. What I am referring to is just as important a necessity to a full life.

Hint: Its ancient Hawaiian name is *hooponopono*. Another hint: It played an important role in the teachings of Jesus. Final hint: If you despise somebody, bear a grudge against them, or feel animosity toward them, you are causing physical problems within your own body. When you realize this and you decide to correct the situation and feel love instead of hate, such a shift in your feelings is impossible unless you go through this.

Of course we are talking about forgiveness.

Forgiveness can be given and received at the subjective level. Daydreaming about your pesky neighbor and seeing yourself forgiving him and in turn being forgiven by him is real. It is as real as going over to his front door, ringing the bell and, when he opens the door, extending your hand in let-bygones-be-bygones forgiveness.

In fact, subjective forgiveness has more advantages than just avoiding a visit. It reaches more deeply inside the person all the way to that person's higher self, and indeed to your higher self as well. That is because it is a right brain activity, which makes it connected to the invisible creative realm where we all came from and to which, thanks to the right brain, we are all still connected.

Another advantage is that when you forgive your whole family, you can save time by letting one uncle stand in for all your uncles, so by forgiving that uncle, you are effectively forgiving all of your uncles. By letting one male cousin stand in for all of your male cousins, you forgive all of your male cousins by forgiving just this one cousin, and so on.

This means that in less than five minutes, you can forgive and be forgiven by not only your entire family but your neighbors, colleagues, and friends as well.

Can you imagine the load that will be lifted from the cells, tissues, and organs of your body? Can you sense the giant step toward purity of consciousness that it will take you? Can you imagine how much easier it will be for the genies, angels, and good fairies to reach you with their blessings—how much wealthier you will be and how much longer you are likely to live?

This Action Plan for forgiving everybody you have ever known will be conducted in one of the rooms in the Universal House of Wisdom. It is the room marked "Telephone." You will be given a list of family member categories. You need choose only one person in that category and realize in the forgiving process that all others in that category are involved.

If you are forgiving your Grandmother on your mother's side and she is deceased, go through the process with her anyhow. It completes the relationship in a wholesome way.

Again, you may have somebody in rapport with you read the instructions. If you are ready to expunge your body and mind from the pollution of past human relationships through forgiveness, you may begin.

ACTION PLAN

for Forgiving Everybody

1. Relax.
2. Daydream.
3. With the doorway enveloped in your bright white light, walk in.
4. Go to the garden and get your key from the drop of water in one of the roses that reflects all the colors.
5. Proceed to the Universal House of Wisdom and, once inside, enter the room marked "Telephone." Leave the door open, be seated, and face that door.
6. First to enter is your grandfather on your father's side. Rise, ask to be forgiven for all misunderstandings, and in turn forgive him. Imagine a hug or handshake as confirming the acceptance of mutual forgiveness. He leaves; you feel elation.
7. Next to enter is your grandmother on your father's side. Go through the same mutual forgiveness with her. She leaves. Follow the same procedure for these others:
8. Grandfather on your mother's side.
9. Grandmother on your mother's side.
10. Father.
11. Mother.
12. One uncle for all of your uncles.
13. One aunt for all of your aunts.
14. One lover for all of your lovers.

15. One brother for all of your brothers.

16. One sister for all of your sisters.

17. One male cousin for all of your male cousins.

18. One female cousin for all of your female cousins.

19. One son for all of your sons.

20. One daughter for all of your daughters.

21. One nephew for all of your nephews.

22. One niece for all of your nieces.

23. One neighbor for all of your neighbors.

24. One teacher for all of your teachers.

25. One business colleague for all of your colleagues.

26. One friend for all of your friends.

27. If there is anybody you need to forgive who is not part of any of these categories, let that person enter now.

28. There is still an important person to come: Yourself. See yourself enter now, taller than usual. Ask to be forgiven by yourself for all the times of poor self-image or self-esteem. In turn, forgive yourself. Give yourself a hug.

29. Leave your key with one of the roses in the garden.

30. Pass through the doorway, leaving it open. Pause and mentally affirm, "My consciousness is one with universal consciousness. Universal life energy surges through me as I go forth."

31. Open your eyes, exclaiming, "Wide awake!"

Congratulations. You have cleansed yourself in the ultimate way and paved the way for future relationships on a higher personal level.

YOUR MIND DEMONSTRATES STAGGERING ABILITIES THAT DEFY SCIENCE

The brain is a marvelous organ made up of thirty billion components and comprising trillions of atoms all working for your intelligence.

The mind is an even more marvelous organ. It has no components and no atoms, but it communicates to the brain and to other minds. Our mind's consciousness seems to contact the consciousness of other people's minds as if we were part of the same larger consciousness.

But the part that boggles our understanding is how our mind contacts what appears to be a universal mind, obtaining from it hard intelligence and miraculous solutions. Daydreaming the Fairyland City route triggers exactly that.

A young woman needed an escort to take her to the important social event of the year. She daydreamed in our special way, seeing herself there. Within two days, an old friend she had not heard from for a long while called and asked to take her.

A freelance teacher needed more outlets for his special courses. He daydreamed and saw them opening up to him. Within two weeks, he had three offers from schools and institutions for his special services.

A forty-five-year-old widow was told by doctors she had what was usually a terminal disease. Her daydreaming involved fixing up the health problem. Within eight months, she no longer had any sign of the disease, and she remarried.

When you relax deeply and daydream assuredly, you activate a larger mind to manifest that daydream. Fairyland City acts as an intermediary. There are other intermediaries as well.

The Silva Method training, now with ten million graduates in 100 countries, uses an imaginary laboratory as an intermediary.

The Christian religions use Jesus as an intermediary, while in Buddhist countries like Tibet, Buddha is usually the intermediary.

Fairyland City is a wondrous intermediary. Its various facilities give you special places for special needs.

It so happens there is a special event going on in Fairyland City right now that you might want to attend. It is called the Carnival of Life. Attend now and you boost your luck.

If you have a few minutes now, I'll take you there.

THE MANY FACES OF LUCK AND HOW TO ATTRACT THEM ALL

Everybody can use better luck. You're late for a train or plane—it's late too, so you make it. What luck!

You meet somebody at a party. You fall in love. You marry. What luck! You might never have met were it not for the party.

You have a hunch about a certain stock. You buy. In six months, it triples in value. Is it because you're a skilled investor? Don't kid yourself. It's just plain luck.

We are now going to Fairyland City, where a carnival is in progress. You'll enjoy the games of chance and you'll be amazed at your luck—luck that you can take home with you.

ACTION PLAN

for Improving Your Luck

1. Relax.

2. Daydream.

3. Envelope the doorway in bright light and walk in.

4. Go to the garden and get your key from the drop of water in one of the roses that reflects all the colors.

5. Go to the rear of the Universal Bank. There you see a big sign: "Carnival of Life." It is going on now.

6. There is a big wheel of fortune. Give it a try. First, visualize winning. Spin it. You have won!

7. There is a penny-pitching game. Try your skill. Imagine winning. Again, you have won!

8. Over at this counter, throw a ball and knock down all the bottles and you win a prize. See it first. Go for it.
   Wow, you did it. Luckier and luckier!

9. I'll let you see yourself winning at other games. Envision yourself winning before you start and later collecting your prize.

10. When you are convinced how lucky you have become, leave your key with a red rose in the garden.

11. Pass through doorway, leaving it open. Pause and mentally affirm, "My consciousness is one with universal consciousness and with Lady Luck. Universal life energy surges through me as I go forth."

12. Open your eyes, exclaiming, "Wide awake!"

From now on, to trigger good luck, pause and see it happening. See the next mail delivery containing good news. See yourself the big winner before starting your poker game. See yourself getting along famously with a special member of the opposite sex. Give your good luck free rein to come in any form. Know that it's already on the way.

SCIENTISTS GIVE OFFICIAL RECOGNITION TO THE ENERGY OF CONSCIOUSNESS

In 1975, a group of about 200 scientists met in Monte Carlo to share their research on the energy of consciousness. This was the second World Psychotronic Conference, the original conference having taken place in Budapest two years before.

I was at the Monte Carlo Conference and observed scientists moving objects with the energy of their consciousness, detecting information at a distance, and lowering another person's brain wave frequency.

In one film, a group of scientists attempted to replicate the phenomenon of table tipping common at séances. They invented an entity named George and beseeched George to confirm his presence by moving the table.

Apparently George demurred for quite a while, but then the table started to move. The scientists became quite excited and exhorted George louder and with more enthusiasm. The table tipped this way and that way and soon began to roll around the room on its edge. The scientists had to scramble out of the way while the camera kept capturing the amazing sight.

There were scores of scientists from the then-USSR. They demonstrated psychokinesis (moving objects with the mind), hypnotism at a distance, and Kirlian photography (photographing the colors of the human aura). However, two years later, at the third World Psychotronic Conference in Tokyo, they were absent. Apparently, there was a tightening up in the Soviet Union of this type of information.

I presented a paper at the Tokyo Conference on the effect of self-hypnosis on learning ability. This was a step in the direction of my receiving the first doctorate ever awarded in psychotronics. I received it from a California university authorized by that state's department of education to give such degrees.

Would you like to feel your own psychotronic energy? Read over these instructions. Then put the book down and do it.

Psychotronic Energy Exercise

- Lift your left arm chest high, palm open and facing to the right. Lift your right arm to the same height, fingers pointing at your left palm, but at least a foot away. Now, keeping them pointed at your left palm, slowly move your right hand's fingers up and down. Move them slowly or you will

fan the air. Be aware of your left palm as you
move your right hand's fingers up and down.
Something is tickling your left palm. It is your
energy of consciousness, psychotronic energy.

Where your consciousness goes, this energy goes,
even if you are working on a problem on the other side
of the world. Can you imagine the power of Universal
Consciousness that fills all space? That energy of consciousness was strong enough to create the universe.
And it did!

FIVE PSYCHOLOGICAL BLOCKS TO GOOD LUCK YOU CAN REMOVE

Earlier, we did some exercises to remove pollutants we
acquire that interfere with invisible support reaching
you.

There are also psychological blocks that we develop
the habit of having. These, too, interfere with your psychotronic energy going out to create and with invisible
creative energy reaching you.

You cannot be an effective metaphysician unless you
remove these five psychological blocks. First, let me list
them. Then, I will tell you how to dump them, literally!

Pessimism. You have little expectation of success, so
you prove yourself right by failing. You have little
hope for a bright tomorrow, so the world obliges.

Limited Self-Esteem. You do not think enough of
yourself, so life short-changes you. You don't get
enough out of life. Your limited self-image limits
your accomplishments.

Self-Hate. Sometimes limited self-esteem turns to actual self-hate. You become a receptacle for your own blame, disdain, and recrimination.

Fear. This is an insidious block. It eclipses light and love. You telegraph your fear to others. Even animals sense it—especially human animals. You become their prey.

Anxiety. Worry causes tension in the body and starvation in the soul. It's like spitting in the face of your guardian angel. Is there any wonder that it leads to health problems ranging from headaches to heart attacks!

I am going to take you on an enjoyable mental trip. It is not to Fairyland City, because it is something you can do for yourself. You did not have any outside help acquiring these psychological blocks, so you don't need any help from the invisible world to divest yourself of them.

You do need to relax. So, read these instructions, and then relax in your usual way. You can have a member of your family or a friend read this Action Plan to you.

ACTION PLAN

to Rid Yourself of Psychological Blocks

1. Deepen your relaxation by counting backwards from 10 to 1.

2. Daydream that you have walked to a lake and there is a canoe on it.

3. You decide to enjoy a boat ride, so you push out the canoe and climb in.

4. You pick up the paddle and start to stroke the water.

5. The canoe feels weighted down and difficult to paddle. You see why. There are big ballast bags in the bow.

6. You reach forward and pick up the first bag. You see it is labeled ANXIETY. You toss it overboard. It makes a big splash!

7. You paddle again. It is easier, but still harder than it should be. You reach for the next bag. It is labeled FEAR. Splash!

8. Continuing on, you realize the going is still too hard. Grabbing the next bag, labeled PESSIMISM, you toss it overboard. Splash!

9. Now your canoe ride is becoming more enjoyable, but it could be still easier to paddle with less weight. You reach for the next bag. It is labeled SELF-HATE. Away with it. Splash!

continued

10. Now you are speeding along. There is only a light breeze, but the canoe is acting as if there is a head wind. It must be that last bag. You reach for it. It is labeled LIMITED SELF-ESTEEM. Splash!

11. Now you enjoy a beautiful canoe ride. You skim the water. It is a beautiful day. Life is easier. Open your eyes, affirming, "Wide awake!"

The canoe trip is symbolic of the ride through life. You are now free of the pollutants to a full life: fear, anxiety, pessimism, self-hate, and limited self-esteem. This does not mean you are free forever. Should you let yourself be polluted in the future, forgive yourself and then take another canoe trip.

You are admired in Fairyland City for doing this. Listen. Can you hear them applauding you?

HOW TO USE LIGHT TO WORK FOR YOU

In the beginning, there was light. And light remains an important element of this created universe, as well as the creative realm.

Remember that you bathe the doorway with light whenever you enter Fairyland City. Light is a common element of creativity and the created, so it acts as a link between the two.

There is no power of darkness. There is only a power of light. Eleanor Roosevelt said, "It is better to light a candle than to curse the darkness." In metaphysics, we do the candle one better: we light up the sky.

We will discuss how light provides us with impenetrable protection when we are under metaphysical attack. But now we will begin to use the light in other positive ways.

Light Exercises

Suppose you are alone and feel uneasy. Here is how to use light to correct that situation.

1. Relax.
2. Visualize the room you are in. Make it more brightly lit than it is.
3. Imagine you have a rheostat. By turning it clockwise, it makes the room brighter still.
4. Turn the rheostat clockwise, making the room burst with brilliant white light.
5. Keep turning the rheostat, making the light more and more brilliant, and feeling the light as a warm, protective love around you.
6. You may end your session leaving the light on, or you may return the rheostat back to its original position.
7. Either way, when you open your eyes, you feel safer and more protected than you ever felt before.

Now that you know the power of this light, you can make it work for you in many ways. Right now, it is helping you connect to Fairyland City by keeping the doorway illuminated by your light.

How about surrounding your car with brilliant white light? It will not enable you to drive it carelessly, but it will add a safety factor when you are in it.

If a person is argumentative, or challenges your authority on the job, or uses debasing language, immediately surround that person with brilliant white light. It will soften the situation. You might even get a quick apology.

Is there a member of the opposite sex with whom you would like to have a closer rapport? Surround that person with your light. Any questions?

Applications are limitless. There are no instances where the use of the white light of your imagination is contraindicated. It helps when you get a haircut, are examined by a physician, take your car to a mechanic, go shopping, eat at a restaurant, and so on.

Sometimes the most positive people go through a depressed period. That is when light becomes intensely important to you. You should make every effort then to bring light into your life not only in the metaphysical way just now discussed but also in physical ways.

Here are some of the physical ways.

- Use white or brightly colored dishes at mealtime.
- Be outdoors as much as possible on sunny days.
- Wear white or brightly colored clothing.
- Switch to white night clothes and bedding.
- Keep some lights on after dark.
- Go without a hat.
- Keep all shades up, venetian blinds open, and curtains parted in the office and at home.
- Associate with positive, enthusiastic, and enlightened people.

HOW TO USE LOVE
TO WORK FOR YOU

This is a topic that will appear from time to time in the chapters ahead. Love, together with light, provides the adhesive that holds this universe together as one. Of the two, love is like a powerful force of attraction, even more powerful than the law of gravity.

Let light be a transmitter of love. Whenever you surround somebody or something with light, let love go with it.

Love is the telephone line that makes all contacts with others a two-way conversation.

Think about love before you start the next chapter. Send light and love to somebody who needs it.

Love yourself as I love you.

4

HOW TO USE THE UNIVERSAL BANK FOR AWESOME RICHES

A Chicago woman was invited to lead spiritual sessions in southern France for six months. She needed her airfare. She asked me to go to the Universal Bank to see if the spiritual nature of her trip would make her eligible for a grant. I agreed to try on her behalf. Within ten days, she received a gift for three-fourths of the needed airfare.

She will manage the rest, but I will not know until she returns what it was about the venture that warranted only a partial endorsement by the Universal Bank.

Perhaps the answer lies in some fairy tale that points out that particular criterion for the Universal Bank's actions. If so, I have not found it in Chinese myths about the Great Chinese Dragon that rises out of the deep earth and, like the Kundalini Serpent, activates our higher centers toward reaching total fulfillment in loving awareness.

Nor have I found it in the Norse legends of sea monsters, or the Biblical sea leviathans, or Swedish whale tales. The sea has always been the symbol of consciousness, and under the sea, the subconscious.

In the tales of Merlin the magician, all the money needed was manifested every time. What was his secret? I did not owe this woman an explanation of why she received only three-fourths of her requirements. What I did tell her was that she should not demand instant total cash from the Universal Bank but rather she should show some trust in it the way the Bank shows trust in her.

HOW TO RAISE YOUR CREDIT STANDING WITH THE UNIVERSAL BANK

This particular woman had a focused goal in her life of helping people through a certain religious approach. Because her goal was aligned with my own, albeit along a different path, I could not refuse her request for help via the Universal Bank.

You may wish to assist others by using your pass to Fairyland City; that is up to you. To use it for others whose goals are not at least parallel to yours would be a breach of trust and might cause your suspension of privileges.

What are your goals? I don't mean like paying the monthly bills, finding a mate, or traveling. Rather, it is the goal you need to affirm or identify as your life goal. A life goal is what you consider your chief purpose in life to be.

Suppose you were Credit Manager at the Universal Bank. How would you rate the following people for credit standing based on their life goals?

Mark: Life goal to become a Hollywood star.

Greg: Life goal to become a multi-patented inventor.

Sara: Life goal to own her own taxi.

Hannah: Life goal to be a loving wife and mother.

Jason: Life goal to be a famous author.

I asked how you would rate them. I did not offer to rate them for you. But let's go through the process together in the same order in which they are listed.

Mark's desire to be a Hollywood star expresses a need to be loved. Of course, it is important to be loved. But by millions? This is a self-centered goal rather than a Creator-centered goal. There is a measure of "putting out" to please people, which deserves merit. So on the credit chart—low to medium.

Greg's desire to be an inventor and the holder of numerous patents expresses the goal of making this a better world to live in. On the face of it, Greg would rate the highest credit available, but because he expresses it in terms of patents, the goal becomes a pecuniary one. Ben Franklin never patented the Franklin Stove or any other of his inventions because he wanted these improvements in the quality of life to be available to as many people as possible. Greg gets—medium.

Sara's life goal to own her own taxi is understandable, but quite individual and quite limited. It gets limited credit.

Hannah's appears to be limited also. But in its creative aspect, motherhood and wifehood are two of the most limitless goals available to womankind. Limitless credit.

Jason wants to be a famous author. This needs to be clarified. It could be as self-centered a goal as Sara's. This would be so if there was no high purpose to the writing. Romance, adventure novels, and mysteries all would probably rate only limited credit in the eyes of the Universal Bank Credit Manager. However, novels with an inner lesson in living or that instill a stronger knowledge of the Creator and levels of intelligence likely merit higher credit limits; how-to books or biographies that depict success formulae or spiritual paths are usually well appreciated by the Creator as well.

Here is a summary of the qualities of life goals that lead to a good Universal Bank credit standing.

- Your desire to break out of strict boundaries and explore new frontiers.
- Your desire to not only make a better life for yourself but make this a better world to live in.
- Your desire to make the best of what exists, do things differently in the future, and never, never quit.

- Your desire to follow inspiration and guidance from Higher Intelligence as you proceed.
- Your desire to look positively at life, and to help others as well as yourself.

THE DEGREE OF PERSONAL NEEDS THAT MIGHT BE MET BY THE UNIVERSAL BANK

Personal needs vary from mosquito repellents to new houses, help mates to soul mates, rent money to buy-out capital.

To keep things simple, it would seem that to talk about money would fit the Universal Bank guidelines. But, quite to the contrary, it is less the money than what the money will be used for.

If this begins to sound like we may be talking about consciousness rather than gifting fairies, angelic credit managers, and money magicians, you are beginning to see the light.

I am beginning to have an acute attack of scientific parameters. Let me quote one scientist whose career spans both technical and psychological sciences, Dr. Willis Harmon, president of the Institute of Noetic Sciences. He says, "Ultimately the reality behind the phenomenal world is contacted not through the physical senses but through the deep intuition. Consciousness is not the end-product of material evolution; rather, consciousness was here first!"

So, scientifically speaking, since consciousness is a primal creative force, by believing in a Universal Bank, we prove its reality. We not only prove its reality, but by the nature of our consciousness, we define the nature of its Credit Manager and its out-payment guidelines.

You and I not only create Fairyland City and its wondrous facilities by imagining it, we create the very gifts that we go there to receive.

CREATING REALLY BIG RESULTS

Now don't get jittery. Even though your consciousness is deeply involved, the magic of consciousness is amazing. You know as little about your own consciousness as you do about the moon or the stars.

When Dr. Carl Simonton first taught psychoneuroimmunology to his civilian cancer patients in Houston, they were so shocked about how the success depended on their personal use of their own consciousness that three-fourths left before the sessions began.

Your admittance to Fairyland City is assured.

Your success at the Universal Bank, the Universal House of Wisdom, and other power sources in that City is assured.

But success is a relative factor. Success can be merely impressive. Success can be absolutely phenomenal. I am interested in moving you up the ladder of success. I want you to be able to realize success that is absolutely phenomenal every time.

How do you get along with your neighbors? No, I am not changing the subject. I am making an essential point. Neighbors usually get along with each other, but here are some factors that might prevent a real neighborly closeness.

If a family wears unusual clothes, that's a hindrance to getting really close to other people. Or if they have strange hairdos, keep a pickup truck out front, go to a different place of worship, have different color skin, speak a different language, or follow a different cultural way of life.

In other words, if your neighbors are strikingly different than you are, you might not be able to relate to them easily.

Would you believe that the Creator behaves in somewhat the same way toward you? The less godlike you are, the less support you have in the invisible realm!

That's quite an order—to become godlike. What are the Creator's qualities? And how do you acquire them?

We all have intuitive knowledge of right and wrong; of loving and non-loving; of being part of the solution or part of the problem; of being positive or negative; of being creative or destructive; of being helpful or hindering.

So, we all have at least an intuitive idea of what kind of a person we should be in order to be more creatorlike. If you still need help in seeing the creatorlike person, use some spiritual leader like Jesus, Buddha, or Mohammed. What were their qualities? How much do you think their line of credit was at the Universal Bank?

OTHER BONUSES THAT COME WITH A HIGHER LINE OF CREDIT

I was teaching in Hong Kong, and decided to rest in my hotel room during the lunch hour. Lying on my bed, I suddenly sat upright.

The thought, "Something is happening to your seminar outline, notes, and manual!" filled my head.

I jumped up, left the room, rang for the elevator, and went directly to the lecture hall. Sure enough, my material was not where I had left it.

I left the room, asking mentally where it was. I automatically walked rapidly down the hotel corridor, turned a corner, and stopped in front of an office. It was the hotel's office to help business people.

I walked in. There was a secretary behind a desk. As I approached her, I saw a copy machine behind her, and in it were my lecture materials. As I explained to her that those papers had been misappropriated from me, a student walked in and shamefacedly admitted the deed.

Note what I did not have to do. I did not have to go to Fairyland City. I did not have to be the least suspicious that an underhanded act might take place. I did not have to ask for any person's help. It all was done for me. Need you ask by whom?

There is an intelligence out there that never sleeps. The more of its traits you emulate, the more this intelligence acts as an adjunct to your intelligence. You enjoy countless "coincidences," endless "synchronicities," and multifarious "serendipities."

At any particular time, wherever you are turns out to be Fairyland City.

A SIMPLE SOUND THAT ATTUNES YOU TO THE CREATOR

"I am as I am," you say. "How can I change into the image of someone I am not?"

A person may have to go through a number of "step-up transformations" to become something bigger than he or she thinks they are.

If we were talking about climbing the ladder of material success, these step-up transformations would likely be schools and colleges or other educational facilities. But we are talking about climbing the ladder of spiritual success. Facts, knowledge, and figures are not involved; time and distance are not involved. What is involved is mind or consciousness.

How long does it take to change your mind? No time at all. Time is not involved. How far can you extend your consciousness? As far as you need to. Distance is not involved. Make the mental decision and it is done.

The simplest step-up transformation would be one that is partially in the material realm, which makes it easy for you and me to relate to, and partially energy or consciousness, which makes it effective in the spiritual realm.

Such a step-up transformer is a special sound. It is spelled O-M. It sounds like O-M-E, rhyming with "home."

Om is called the universal sound, or mantra. It deserves this title because it does indeed have universal significance. If the universe made a sound—that is, if the galaxies made a sound as they turned, and if our solar system made a sound, and if these macrocosmic sounds were mixed with the microcosmic sounds of electrons spinning around their atomic nuclei and molecules vibrating—the closest the human voice can come to imitating that sound is Om when chanted in a long, drawn-out O-O-O-M-M-M.

Everything vibrates to this universal sound. If you could Om long enough, you would hear this vibration in the room. Use a loudspeaker with the volume turned up and there will be no doubt of this.

Place your arms straight out in front of you, palms down, and, when you intone the sound Om, you will feel a tingle in your palms that is your skin vibrating.

That's the microcosmic aspect of the sound. The larger and more spiritual macrocosmic aspect of the sound is its attunement to the universe. By sounding Om, you get on the Universe's wavelength, so to speak. By being on the Creator's wavelength, you can be closer neighbors.

Practice the sound Om now. Let the "O" part last about three times longer than the "M" sound. Take a deep breath before you begin so that you can Om for at least seven seconds. Start with your mouth open a bit wider than it needs to be. This adds an "OW" sound at the beginning, which is how the Hindu Tibetan spiritual practitioners sound it.

After practicing to intone the mantra Om, begin to use it one to three times a day to heighten your spiritual attunement. Here is how.

ACTION PLAN

Using the Mantra "Om"
for Spiritual Attunement

1. Sit in a comfortable chair where you have both visual and audio privacy.

2. Close your eyes, take a deep breath, and exhale.

3. Think of the vast universe and its Creator for a few seconds.

4. Out of respect for the Creator and the created, take a deep breath and Om aloud, prolonging it as long as is comfortable.

5. Repeat twice, Om-ing a total of three times.

6. Open your eyes and sit quietly for a minute or two.

The total elapsed time for this Action Plan is certainly no more than three or four minutes. It has an impact on you. It also has an impact on the universe. You both mean more to each other. The universe becomes a stronger invisible means of support to you, and you become a more dependable co-creator. Your credit just rose at the Universal Bank.

SOME TIPS ON THE USE OF
THE UNIVERSAL BANK

Have you noticed at your personal bank that when you stand in line awaiting an available teller, a camera is photographing you? This, of course, is so that the bank can have a record of who was there in case of a robbery or other untoward event.

There is no such camera at the Universal Bank. This is because the Bank already knows who you are; in fact, it has a whole dossier about you. It is on a page devoted entirely to you in the Book of Life. Furthermore, you don't have to stand in line to wait for a teller. The Bank's administrator already knew that you were coming, as well as all the others, and had the teller windows staffed accordingly. Banking hours? None exist.

Such is the nature of Higher Intelligence in the invisible realm. Even *Star Trek* is made to look elementary.

Suppose you feel like a trip to Las Vegas. Games of chance, throwing dice, and pulling the slot machine handles give you a thrill. It's not a cheap thrill—it takes money, more than you can put your hands on right now. So you decide to cash a check at the Universal Bank.

You follow the procedure to enter Fairyland City. You go to the Universal Bank. To your astonishment, it is closed. Didn't that fellow Stone say it was always open? (No. He said there were no banking hours.) Time does not exist in this invisible realm, but other limits that are not physical do indeed exist.

Like motive.

Your motive for going to the Universal Bank to obtain money for gambling is a no-no. Sorry. The Bank is closed.

In my own experience, the Universal Bank has nothing against Las Vegas. In fact, I have found that Las Vegas may be temporarily used as a branch office by the Universal Bank.

Ted, a friend of mine, needed to buy a new car. His old car was faced with huge repair bills in order to keep it running dependably. He went to the Universal Bank and cashed a check for the needed amount. As you might expect, the cash you actually receive at the Universal Bank is imaginary cash. It later materializes.

After a few days, Ted told me he had a sudden desire to go to Las Vegas for the weekend. He phoned me when he returned. He won an amount equal to the check he had cashed at the Universal Bank.

A general rule to follow in making withdrawals from the Universal Bank is that need, not greed, is the motive behind it.

The need can be for basic survival, but it does not have to be a matter of life or death. You can cash a check to pay off burdensome bills.

Money materializes.

You can cash a check to pay for university tuition. The Bank is all for increased knowledge and awareness.

Money materializes.

You can cash a check to pay for a trip to visit dear relatives. The Bank likes to help with relationships.

Money materializes.

"Nothing happened," complained Lorraine. "I cashed a check to pay my neighbor's real estate taxes."

"I don't make excuses for the Universal Bank," I replied. "Why don't you just ask the Universal Bank?"

Lorraine did. She received an answer. "I got the idea that I was depriving my neighbor of a lesson she needed to learn. Did I make that up?"

I had heard that answer before. My reply was easy. "No, you did not make that up."

When it comes to solving life's problems, we need to use both sides of our brain. We use the logical left side to seek out the particular knowledge that helps us toward a solution. We use the intuitive, creative right side to connect us to the wisdom that permeates the cosmos.

When the right side, through imagination, seeks the answer, the answer comes. What you visualize, believe, and expect then materializes.

It could be changes from abnormality to normality in your body, as with cyberphysiology. Health materializes.

It could be a goal that needs to be reached, as with the Silva Method's laboratory. The goal is reached.

It could be a money problem resolved, as with Fairyland City's Universal Bank. The money manifests.

Consciousness, via the imagination, creates.

HOW TO KEEP MONEY FLOWING TO YOU

Do you have a skill or talent that is proving to be a valuable asset to you? Have you ever helped others to develop a similar talent?

As a musician, author, poet, or artist, do you feel that by helping another person to get started in your field, you are increasing the competition, which is already stiff?

Here's the answer via a story. A young couple signed a lease in a new community shopping center for their new shoe store. Business was terrible. They were financed adequately to last out those first six months to a year, which any new business must be prepared to do. But at the end of a year, they were a long way from making a living.

When they heard that two vacant stores in the shopping center were also just leased to shoe companies, they threw their hands up. This was the last straw. How could three businesses show a profit when even one was in the red? They decided to relocate.

While they were looking for another site for their shoe business, a funny thing began to happen. The other stores had opened and now their own store began to thrive. They realized that where their own store attracted only a few shoe customers, three shoe stores attracted ten times as many shoe customers. Moral: The more the merrier.

I have assisted many would-be authors to become published authors. And my royalties rose. The same can be true for any gifted person who helps another to develop a similar talent.

Are you exporting? Show me how. Are you franchising? Show me how. Are you advertising successfully? Show me how.

One rule: Don't ask me, or whomever you help, for money. Do your sharing without a fee.

Since I or the person you help does not pay you, the universe must pay you. There is no way to be creative, productive, or helpful without your receiving your just reward. Since recipients are not taking care of you, the universe automatically takes care of you.

And the universe pays much higher than union wage.

If you do not have a special talent, skill, or ability to share with others, all is not lost. Here are some other possibilities.

- Be a part-time companion to a senior citizen.
- Read for a blind person.
- Join a fraternal or service organization.
- Volunteer your time at a nearby hospital.
- Tutor a foreign-born person in English.
- Stay overtime voluntarily at work to expedite a project.
- Do more at work than you are expected to do.
- Donate food or other useful material to a charity.

Depending on the substantiality of your sharing, you may receive surprise gifts. Lisa received a valuable antique from an aging collector she assisted. Andrew won a lottery after he helped a family to move.

Or, good things may happen to you, a sort of serendipity. A long-forgotten loan may be repaid. Or you may receive an unexpected tax refund. Or an uncle whom you never really knew may bequeath a sizable sum.

Consider these all as payments to you by the universe, through the Universal Bank, for value received.

There is nobody whom you can help that is outside this universal reciprocity.

We are all one.

BEING ONE OF THE GOOD GUYS
ASSURES YOUR CONTINUED
MEMBERSHIP IN FAIRYLAND CITY

There's a gangster film. There's a chase. The bad guys are captured and the good guys win in the end.

There's a novel about the innocent widow being compromised by the plotting villain. She is rescued by the hero. Again, the good guys win in the end.

The theme is the same in all the media, from nursery rhymes and fairy tales to detective stories and operas.

But it goes even further than that. It is not only an American theme, it is an international theme. It is not only a visible realm theme, it is an invisible realm theme, too.

Bad guys are barred entry into Fairyland City. Good guys have a life membership.

You have already received your life membership in Fairyland City; you have access to all of its magic. That's because you are a good guy.

There are hypnotic forces in this material, visible world that try to program us in the wrong direction. You need to be aware of these negative forces and do some counterprogramming in order to maintain your status as a good guy.

Here are some of the forces to watch out for, and what to do about it should you find that one or more has its clutches on you.

> *Greed.* Money is a great seducer. One does not have to rob or steal to be a bad guy. Just raising prices unnecessarily, or being overly stingy, could raise some eyebrows in the invisible realm.

Pomposity. There are no special people. The good
   guys are everyday people. If somebody acts supe-
   rior, they are in for a comedown. And it can hurt.

Sexual aggressiveness. Bodily pleasures are habit-
   forming. Sometimes the physical chemistry
   between the sexes is "impossible" to resist—
   and somebody gets hurt.

Of course, these three are only the beginning. But you
know the rest of the story.

What you might not know is what to do about it.
How do you program *out* these unwanted bad guy forces
and program *in* the ability to behave appropriately?

Use your mental computer. The visible, material
world is programming you all the time by getting to
your mental computer. You can use it, too.

You are having your morning cup of coffee. You have
heard the news. Next comes the weather, but first an
announcement. "Golden Cream is the richest ice cream
you can enjoy. It scoops smooth, spoons smooth, tastes
smooth." You might not even be paying attention, but
the next time you buy ice cream, you become part of the
statistics that prove it pays to advertise.

Before the day is over, you will have been bombarded
by television commercials, radio blurbs, newspaper ads,
bus placards, and billboards. Cake mixes will be held by
attractive models; chocolate will be offered by friendly,
irresistible hands, beer will be set before you in such a
way that it is an obvious truth: Beer and love go hand in
hand. All is programming.

It wouldn't be so bad if this uninvited and unwanted
programming was limited to product purchasing. Ideas
that affect morals, beliefs, and behavior are being

slipped to us twenty-four hours a day and escape our critical faculties. So, they are more insidious.

It all adds up to a monumental invasion of our minds that can render us unworthy of membership in Fairyland City.

So what do we do about it?

We can program ourselves in two ways. Both ways involve relaxing deeply. Once relaxed, we can use words stated mentally, or pictures seen mentally.

We are going to take you to a Magic Mirror in the next chapter. It is in Fairyland's House of Wisdom. There you will learn how to reprogram yourself with mental pictures. Right now we will learn to reprogram ourselves using words said mentally.

There are three steps, two of which you already know: 1. Relax, 2. Auto-suggest, 3. End. You already know how to relax and you already know how to end your relaxation session. But how does one use auto-suggestion?

An auto-suggestion is like new data for your mental computer. Since your mental computer believes you, it is like acquiring new behavior and even new beliefs.

PROTECTING YOURSELF AGAINST UNWANTED INFLUENCES

You lost your temper and struck a member of your family. It is not like you to do this, yet you did it. How do you use auto-suggestion to assure that you will hereinafter be in control of your temper and not resort to violence?

Auto-suggestion is talking to your self. Your self is your mind. Your mind passes the thought to your brain. Your brain is your computer that runs you. It accepts the auto-suggestion and runs you accordingly.

Talk to yourself right now. Say, "I don't like cake." Do it now, silently or aloud. Now repeat. Again. Once more.

You have said it four times. Of course, you still like cake. But I'll bet you don't like it more than you did a minute ago, and very likely, the next time you face up to cake, you'll remember this moment. You might even hesitate.

The basic technique for using auto-suggestion is to relax so deeply that both sides of your brain are exposed to the instructions given in the auto suggestion.

Yes, you have been relaxing, but you need to relax even more deeply to reprogram your mental computer effectively.

Sorry to throw more methodology at you, but you need to know some additional deepening techniques if you wish to protect yourself against such unwanted influences as:

- Advertisements for fattening and health-sapping foods.
- Propaganda to induce you to smoke.
- Pressures to overindulge in beer and intoxicating liquor.
- Temptations to spend more than you should because of marketing inducements.
- Clever ways to manipulate your mind on political, religious, or personal matters.

Additional Steps for Relaxing

Here are a few additional steps you can add to your Chapter 1 relaxation procedure that will bring you into a deeper level where programming can take place.

- Before you close your eyes, tire them by staring at a spot on the wall you are facing. Don't overdo it. When your lids feel heavy, allow them to close.

- Add countdown time. You can start at 20, 50, or even 100 and count backwards slowly until you reach the count of one.

- Envision more passive, natural, relaxing scenes. Nature provides an abundant supply. Pick scenes you have actually observed in the past.

- Affirm along the way, "Each time I relax in this way, I go deeper, faster."

- Use a descending activity to imagine. Perhaps imagine yourself going down an escalator or a mine shaft or a department store elevator with the public address system announcing what each floor features.

Now for the verbal approach to auto-suggestion.

Words That Reprogram You in the Right Direction

Since we started with "cake," let us continue with auto-suggestion in the realm of food. How do you reprogram your eating habits using words in a deeply relaxed state?

Here are some of the things you can mentally say to change from fattening to less fattening, unhealthy to healthy, and energy-sapping to energy-providing. Food may not be your problem. It is a simple matter to use the same basic approach to other unwanted conditions by changing the words to fit the problem.

To eat less or to eat more correctly, reprogram yourself to the following.

- "I agree to abolish these problem foods (name them). They no longer taste good to me. I am repulsed when they are offered to me."

- "From this time on, I will not be attracted to foods that I have agreed to abolish. I will be perfectly satisfied with foods that I know to be non-fattening and nutritional. This satisfaction will be both emotional and hunger-wise."

- "Just a moderate amount of nutritious food will give me the same satisfaction as when I ate more. I no longer will reach that bloated condition that I have felt after a heavy meal."

- "Whenever I feel hungry in between meals, I will take a deep breath and exhale, knowing that this false hunger will then disappear."

These statements are placed in separate paragraphs and in separate quotes. Together, they are too much to remember and still stay relaxed. So review them one after the other for use singly in separate auto-suggestion sessions.

On the other hand, if you have a friend or family member who is available to read them to you, the reading should include all four statements. The reader should allow time for you to mentally repeat each sentence.

ACTION PLAN

for Reprogramming Yourself against Unwanted Effects

1. Relax.

2. Deepen your relaxation using one or more techniques listed on page 95.

3. Mentally repeat the auto-suggestions given on page 96, one per session, or all if you have assistance.

4. End. Remember to say, "Wide awake, feeling better than before."

PROTECTING YOURSELF AGAINST OTHER UNWANTED EXTERNAL INFLUENCES

The effort to get us to change our eating habits in order to benefit certain food producers is perhaps the mightiest of all controlling campaigns levied against us. So the above procedures have used food as the subject.

However, what if electrical transmission lines are surreptitiously affecting your peace of mind? Are you helpless to restore your own natural serenity? Of course you can do something about it.

In this particular instance, step 3 of your auto-suggestions should be along these lines:

> "I am in control of my peace of mind. I block out all irritating energies that come from unwanted outside sources. My nerve stability, emotional control, and calmness remain strong."

Repeat three times a day for a week or so, then once a day.

Suppose you are temporarily subjected to second-hand smoke. Although tobacco companies disagree, medical research confirms that being in the presence of smokers can be damaging to non-smokers. Help to minimize this damage by programming yourself with these words:

> "I apologize to my lungs for subjecting you to others' smoke. Protect your membranes while this lasts. Let the healing process prevail and let your usual healthy pink condition be unaffected."

You will, of course, add appropriate mental pictures of healthy, pink lungs.

Here is one more example of a possible external influence against which you need reprogramming in order to remain on your chosen track.

People tend to be negative. Are you surrounded by or have repeated contact with people who:

- Talk failure instead of success?
- Warn of non-existing problems?
- Express pessimism persistently?
- Complain or argue as a way of life?
- Are destructive rather than constructive?

If so, here are some protective auto-suggestion commands you may wish to give yourself in order to remain immune from their pollutants to life.

> "Negative thoughts and negative suggestions never have any influence over me. I always maintain a positive approach to life. I am one with the Creator and stay resolute as a positive co-creator."

Not all the negative forces with which people and the environment can bombard us can be enumerated here. It is sufficient that you now have examples of what you can do to neutralize their effects. These approaches can be adapted easily to cover any situation and provide you with means to protect, and through auto-suggestion, program or reprogram your natural state and behavior.

Thank you for participating in your own welfare. Help is now on the way. The Creator helps those who help themselves. You are helping yourself. So you can now avail yourself of the magical support that is yours in Fairyland City.

On the pages ahead, we will not only supply mental pictures to augment your auto-suggestion words, but we will take you on a trip to Fairyland City to acquire invisible support.

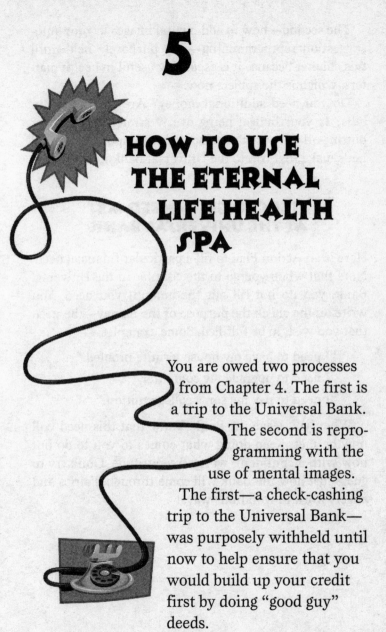

5

HOW TO USE THE ETERNAL LIFE HEALTH SPA

You are owed two processes from Chapter 4. The first is a trip to the Universal Bank. The second is reprogramming with the use of mental images. The first—a check-cashing trip to the Universal Bank— was purposely withheld until now to help ensure that you would build up your credit first by doing "good guy" deeds.

The second—how to add mental images to your auto-suggestion reprogramming—was purposely held until this chapter because it is especially useful in health matters, which is the subject now.

Do you need additional money? Are you behind in bills? Is your budget being overly stretched? Are you putting off the purchase of something important to you? Let's make that trip to the Universal Bank now.

STEPS TO GET A NEED MET AT THE UNIVERSAL BANK

Here is an Action Plan to fill a particular financial need. Note that when you go to the counter in the Universal Bank, you do not fill out the amount you need. You write on the check the purpose of the money—the need that you wish to be fulfilled. Some examples:

"I need to have my house termite-proofed."

"I need to upgrade my computer."

"I need to pay my son's college tuition."

When you leave the Bank, know that this need will now be met. Keep doing what comes to you to do but now with a confident, worry-free attitude. Don't try to guess just how the Bank will come through. Fairies and angels work in wondrous ways!

ACTION PLAN

to Fill Your Need at the Universal Bank

1. Relax.
2. Daydream.
3. With the doorway to Fairyland City enveloped in your bright white light, walk in.
4. Go to the garden and get your key from the drop of water in one of the roses that reflects all the colors.
5. Proceed to the Universal Bank building.
6. Stand out front and contemplate the abundance of the universe.
7. Enter the Universal Bank by climbing the many stone steps to the entrance doorways.
8. Once inside, go to a table and fill out a check, spelling out your need on the check.
9. Walk to the counter and give the check to a smiling teller.
10. Return to the garden, leaving your key with one of the roses.
11. Pass through the doorway, leaving it open and mentally affirming, "My consciousness is one with universal consciousness. Universal life energy surges through me as I go forth."
12. Open your eyes, feeling great. Visualize your need being met. Know that your need will be met.

HOW TO USE VISUALIZATION AND IMAGINATION TO REPROGRAM YOURSELF

Do you want to lose weight? Relax and see yourself thin.

Do you want to be a non-smoker? Relax and visualize yourself free of the habit.

Do you want to help a strained muscle to heal? Relax and see yourself moving normally.

Daydreaming is creative. Control your daydreaming; use it to solve a problem. Seeing the solution to the problem helps to bring about that solution.

All the ways to reprogram yourself using mental words can be just as effective using mental pictures.

Using both mental words and mental pictures in your deeply relaxed state is the most powerful way to change your behavior, and it works by reprogramming your mental computer to behave the way you want, not the way the media wants you to behave.

If you cannot see yourself not biting your nails, not losing your temper, or not being late to work, forget it. This does not mean you have a poor imagination. It means you have poor motivation.

Cathy would blush at the drop of a hat. In a face-to-face situation, her face turned beet red. Knowing it was going to happen brought it on. She became so ashamed of this that she began to avoid people. However, she was not stupid and she was not intent on being a loner. She yearned for a social life, so she decided to do something about it.

She realized she had started to blush as a child. She blushed talking to her parents then. Was this a reaction to persons of authority? It could very well have been exactly that, because she blushed now quite readily with people who were either in authority or could be in authority.

Her programming approach was to use auto-suggestions that reinforced her self-esteem. "I have no reason to feel inferior or to be self-conscious. I may have needed blushing as a child, but it is no longer needed and it is becoming less and less frequent." She saw her face remaining its normal color while talking to men, elders, anybody.

This combination of mental words and mental pictures succeeded in ridding Cathy of this embarrassing behavior. She continued to blush at situations any girl would blush at. She wanted help in reprogramming herself out of this, too, but her friends convinced her to accept what came naturally.

Accidental death does not come naturally. Suppose you got a flyer in the mail that said in big, black letters:

ACCIDENTAL DEATH IS THE NUMBER 1 KILLER OF PEOPLE UNDER 45

You are under 45. You realize you are being programmed to think that accidental death is an odds-on probability for you. As you open the flyer, there is your name at the top, faithfully produced there by the computer and inserted repeatedly in the body of the letter. Zing!

I'll tell you what I would do if the name was mine.

First of all, I would not read the letter. I know that belief in the probability of accidents increases the chance of an accident happening. So, by not reading the letter, I prevent it from being a self-fulfilling prophecy.

Next, I relax to detoxify myself of what the big black letters may have already done to me. After deepening my relaxation, I play a mental movie. I see myself driving safely, getting into the tub or shower safely, walking up and down different stairways safely.

Before opening my eyes, I give myself the following auto-conditioning by mentally telling myself: "I do not fear accidents. I am always cautious and aware. I keep myself safe."

I repeat this three times for emphasis. It is like compensating for those big black letters.

Negative programming can come from many sources besides the communications media. People like to talk to you about their troubles or illnesses. They dump their load on you. You can choose to carry it and suffer with them or at the first opportunity to close your eyes and deny yourself such a load or see yourself free of it.

Events at work can go through a bad spell. Errors, losses, and competition act as ego depressors. If prolonged, they can bring on acute depression and burnout. At best, they can bring on pessimism and despair.

Why am I being negative myself by confronting you with such negative matters? What have these negative matters to do with fairies and angels and magicians—the positive forces in the invisible realm?

The answer might stun you: They act as a barrier to your receiving help from the other side—from the fairies and angels and magicians.

See why I want you to relax and reprogram yourself after every such attack by the visible realm?

YOUR ARTILLERY IN THE BATTLE AGAINST NEGATIVITY

Here are some specific statements and some sharp pictures you can use—one, the other, or both—to reprogram yourself back to your regular positive state when you have been negatively attacked.

Here are four common areas of possible negative pitfalls and what you can do about them, followed by one that is a general catch-all.

Pessimism

Words. "I am a pessimist. I worry. When I open my eyes, I will no longer be a pessimist. I will be an optimist. I will change from worrying about bad outcomes to expecting successful outcomes." Reinforce the following day like this: "I am no longer a pessimist and a worrier. I am an optimist. I expect successful outcomes."

Picture. Play a movie of a successful tomorrow. Include a clock that shows what is happening each hour. For example, the clock shows 9 A.M. Business is good. Everything is going even better than usual.

Personal Loss

Words. "I survive loss because I am in control. I am becoming calm, emotionally stronger, and more secure. Every day, in every way, I become safer, happier, and more confident."

Picture. See yourself answering questions and helping many people. They come to you because they are attracted by your strength.

Power to Love

Words. "I grow every day in my own self-esteem and self-worth. I am better able to love and be loved. I receive as much love from people as I give to them and to myself."

Picture. See yourself forgiving and being forgiven by the person that has damaged a relationship. Also, see yourself at a party surrounded by loving admirers.

Burn-Out and Loss of Creativity

Words. "I am feeling a new interest and attraction to my work. Every day, I become more enthusiastic." Also, "When I relax, I increase my daily creativity and I get ideas. I solve problems. The invisible realm assists my intelligence with answers and solutions."

Picture. See brilliant light descending from the cosmos and enveloping you in it.

General

Words. "I believe in the creative power of my imagination and visualization. I expect positive results. I am making progress whether I can see it or not. My expectations are high."

Picture. Identify the problem, then change the picture to the solution, the way you want things to be. Mentally hold this solution or picture for a few seconds. Later, during the day, when the problem comes to mind, put the problem out of your mind by recalling your solution picture.

THE KILLER THAT EVERYBODY FACES DAILY

All of the negative programming sources mentioned in this and the previous chapter are potential causes of ill health. They can be bunched under a single heading called STRESS.

Stress is a killer. Especially prolonged stress. It is a known medical fact that prolonged stress lowers a person's white corpuscle blood count. These are the antibodies or "police" that fight germs and comprise either a strong or weak immune system.

Under prolonged stress, a person can easily fall prey to invading bacteria. That's bad enough. But vital organs can begin to fail as they, too, are weakened.

Combating stress is a pleasurable event. Reprogramming and auto-conditioning are pleasurable events. They are physically relaxing and mentally enjoyable.

Any pleasurable event interferes with the deadly effects of stress, but does not tend to erase them, as do reprogramming and auto-conditioning. A study found that a pleasant family celebration can enhance the strength of the immune system for the next two days. Jogging, fishing, or other leisure activities cause an immediate positive response in your immune system, as do pleasant social activities.

At the opposite side, criticism by the boss or frustrating encounters with fellow employees cause some of the biggest setbacks in immune function. So did heavy workloads and impending deadlines. Morbid note: deadlines are self-defined.

When there was a period of three to five days of stressful events, colds became noticeable. The incubation period for a cold is one to three days.

But don't wait to get a cold. Stress does not announce itself but if you suspect that untoward events are putting you under stress, don't wait until your throat is sore or your blood pressure rises or you feel on the edge of a nervous breakdown—relax.

Relax as you learned to do in Chapter 1 as part of your controlled daydreaming. Or, relax as you learned to do in the previous Chapter 4 as part of your procedure for reprogramming, with its valuable deepening techniques.

Relaxation is the antidote to stress.

HOW FAIRYLAND CITY'S ETERNAL LIFE HEALTH SPA CAN HELP YOU HEAL THE EFFECTS OF STRESS

If you are under stress, your reaction to events is your personal responsibility. You cannot be helped to feel pleasure instead of pain.

You can decide to react differently to events so that they are no longer stressful. Or you can remove yourself from the environment in which the stress exists. This, of course, is difficult to impossible for people in such ultra-stressful jobs as air-traffic controllers, police officers, firefighters, et cetera.

If you do neither and find that your health is beginning to suffer, remember that you have a membership in Fairyland City, where miracles in healing occur daily in its Eternal Life Health Spa.

There are exercise machines in the Spa that are excellent therapy for what ails you externally. There is a Pharmacy chock full of balms, tonics, and miracle cures. There is a Magic Mirror on the wall that makes your imaging of internal cures manifest as better health in your body. There is a hot water tub in which, when you pretend you are in this magic Jacuzzi, nerve problems lessen or disappear.

The choice is yours. Use these imaginary facilities as your intuition dictates. I will review how others have used them with success.

Pete had a chronic tennis elbow. He was about ready to give up the game when he was introduced to controlled daydreaming. In just one visit to the Eternal Life Health Spa he was free of this problem. He bought a tennis elbow liniment from its Pharmacy, mentally rubbed it on, and worked out on the tennis machine. He is now playing real tennis.

Nancy had a trick knee. She decided a treadmill would be right for it. Her controlled imagination seemed to help it on her first try. Encouraged, she persisted. After several visits over a period of a week, her knee caused her no more trouble.

As you can see, the Pharmacy stocks your every need. If you are in Fairyland City and enter the pharmacy, you probably have not the faintest idea what you should obtain.

Stop. Ask yourself what you need. Wait for an answer. The answer that comes sounds like one you yourself made up. Don't worry. It's the right answer. (Remember, at this relaxed level, your mind is connected to a Higher Intelligence.)

Once the answer comes, you barely have time to ask for the curative product and it appears in your hand.

The magic Jacuzzi is self-explanatory. But you need help to make fullest therapeutic use of the Magic Mirror on the wall.

A MAGIC MIRROR THAT REFLECTS IMPROVED HEALTH

There is a new medical concept that is fast gaining acceptance among more and more practitioners. It is called cyberphysiology. It states that the mind has a computer-like control over the body. It calls for relaxed mental picturing reinforced by mental affirmation, both words and pictures directed at the ailing part. It goes a giant step beyond what was called psychoneuroimmunology, which referred only to revving up the immune system.

The Eternal Life Health Spa recognized cyberphysiology long before the term was invented. Its Magic Mirror on the wall enhances the creativity of healing mental images.

To use the Magic Mirror on the wall, you relax. You identify your body's ailing organ or tissues and you begin to encourage it to heal. You do not mentally talk like a lion tamer with whip in hand. Instead, you talk apologetically (after all, you caused your health problem by permitting yourself to be stressed or by harboring other negative attitudes) and you talk lovingly, for this part of your body is a dear friend.

You probably do not have a health problem now, so you do not have to perform the Action Plan that is presented now. Let it act as an instruction for any later healing that you may need.

HOW TO USE THE MAGIC MIRROR TO HEAL

We will use a hypothetical case of a broken bone and give the steps to follow for accelerating healing with the assistance of the Magic Mirror on the wall. Precise verbiage will not be given, but you can put the intent in your own words.

Action Plan

for Faster Healing Using the Magic Mirror on the Wall

1. Relax. Remain in bed if you are bedridden.
2. Daydream.
3. Envelop the doorway to Fairyland City with your bright white light and walk in.
4. Go to the garden and get your key from the drop of water in one of the roses that reflects all the colors.
5. Proceed to the building named Eternal Life Health Spa.
6. Pause and think a moment of the source of Eternal Life.
7. Enter the building and imagine a Magic Mirror on the wall in front of you, directly opposite the entrance.
8. Sit in the chair opposite the floor-length Mirror. Look at yourself in the mirror.
9. Turn your awareness to your bone injury. Greet your bone as an old friend. Mentally apologize for the unavoidable mishap.
10. Mentally encourage your bone to heal.
11. Look in the Mirror. You see your bone. As you watch, you see your bone responding to your plea. It is visually beginning to heal.

12. Watch the reflection of your bone in the Mirror as it continues to improve. Like time-lapse photography, the Mirror's reflection shows your bone slowly becoming perfect.

13. See your bone in the Mirror as now perfect. Thank your bone for healing.

14. Leave the Eternal Life Health Spa, pausing to think a moment of the source of eternal life.

15. Return to the garden, leaving your key with one of the roses.

16. Pass through the doorway, leaving it open and mentally affirming, "My consciousness is one with universal consciousness. Universal life energy surges through me as I go forth."

17. Open your eyes, feeling great. Know that your broken bone is healing faster than ever.

CAUSES OF ILLNESS AND HOW TO NEUTRALIZE THEM

As mentioned before, relaxation is the great antidote for stress. It is indeed a fountain of youth.

But what is the antidote for a flat tire that makes you late that in turn causes you to rush up the stairs, lose your balance, fall, and break a bone?

What is the antidote for an explosive argument with a mate, a neighbor, or a colleague that causes you to raise your voice, your pulse, and your blood pressure and places you on the edge of having a stroke or a heart attack?

And what is the antidote for the nervousness before an important meeting that causes you acute pain in your stomach and ulcer-like symptoms?

Nothing said in this book is intended as a substitute for medical attention, but rather as a supplement to it. The best approach of all is to avoid or neutralize the causes of illness so that you don't have to cope with the symptoms or the ultimate effects.

How do you manage to do this?

You enlist help from the other side.

6

HOW TO PROFIT FROM THE UNIVERSAL TRADE CENTER

You might wonder what trade and commerce profit and loss have to do with the other side—the side of fairies, angels, genies, and magicians. The fact is, material exchange is going on constantly in the material world, and participating in it can very likely be part of your function on earth, including, of course, making a living for yourself and your family.

Plants take water and minerals from the earth and return it to the air and the earth. Water evaporates from the earth and seas and returns to the earth and seas as precipitation from the sky. Heat leaves the earth and is replaced by heat from the sun.

To think that this is all outside the realm of the angels is a mistake. As the Creator's helpers, they are expediters, troubleshooters, and facilitators for all creation.

How about when you, as a baker, invest your skill in flour and ovens and sell your bread for a profit? Is this outside the Creator's domain? Of course not. It is circulation.

Circulation is a fundamental characteristic of the universe whether it is a galaxy spinning, the Earth turning, winds blowing, or shirts selling.

That is why when you give of your time or money, asking nothing in return, you receive a return whether you want it or not. It is a natural law.

You and I are part of a single organization that takes care of its own. Everything you see, hear, touch, or smell, separate as it seems, is part of this organization.

One of the best ways to see the unity of all things is to see planet Earth from outer space.

When Astronaut Rusty Schweikert found himself floating outside of the Apollo spacecraft when something went wrong with it in the late 1960s, he looked at planet Earth and saw no boundaries. He felt a oneness with all people on Earth, as well as every living creature and every earthly object.

When you take a long view of your own life, you see the big picture. You are part of one consciousness that permeates the universe.

Scientists used to say that action at a distance was impossible. Now when they separate two electrons that are rotating around the nucleus of an atom and change their orbit, one electron always knows what the other is doing. They remain in symmetry, as if they were perfect mirror images of one another.

The universe is a network of energy fields and material particles. Included in this universal network is human consciousness—your consciousness.

And so it is that your consciousness can tap into the source of all knowledge, and your controlled daydreams can become miraculous recoveries, spontaneous wealth, and magical coincidences.

Can you not love the rest of you? Is it possible for you not to love the intelligent, loving energy we call the universe?

THE UNIVERSAL TRADE CENTER BELONGS TO YOU

For those who take without giving, for those who exploit others for their own gain, and for those who deplete resources without restoring them in kind, Fairyland City is a lie and its Universal Trade Center is a rumor.

The rest of you, follow me.

On your next trip to Fairyland City, you will visit the Universal Trade Center and participate in a barter that will profit you to no small extent.

Give something of value and you will receive something of value. That something could be helping to heal, and receiving a boost in your own health automatically. That something could be making a financial loan, and not only having a universal endorsement, but a bonus above the prescribed interest payment. That something could be coming up with a way to improve the quality of life, and having your own quality of life enhanced manyfold, often in unrelated and unexpected ways.

The fact is the Universal Trade Center belongs to you. Go to Fairyland City, enter the Universal Trade Center, and it is guaranteed that you will receive remuneration for a fair business deal, for a new idea, for an act of consideration, or for a loving gift. There is only one measuring stick: motive.

The higher the selflessness of the motive, the higher the rate of return.

Take healing. If you need personal healing, go to the Eternal Life Health Spa. But if you wish to help another person, go to the Universal Trade Center. Healing usually entails the highest of motives, so you receive a high rate of return. Assuming you are in good health, you will enjoy an even higher level of well-being.

In addition to this personal benefit, there will be a benefit to humanity as a whole. For instance, a surge in people helping to heal other people came with the advent of the Silva Method. This became a spiritual alternative medicine.

Bringing alternative medicine into the mainstream of American health care then took an impressive leap forward with the creation in Washington, D.C. of the Office of Alternative Medicine in 1992. However, the creation turned out to overshadow its subsequent activities as it subsided into just another government office.

It was not until May 1993 that the office sponsored a four-day conference in Washington with the impressive title "Alternative Medicine, Wellness and Health Care Reform: Preparing for a Sustainable Future."

A few notable speeches at that conference spelled out the ideals of alternative medicine. Marilyn Ferguson, publisher of *Brain/Mind Bulletin* and author of *The Aquarian Conspiracy*, predicted that alternative medicine would introduce the next paradigm shift into this society, and that it might be in the direction of service— the only thing that she said unifies the human being and society to the planet.

The Conference moderator, James Gordon, from the Georgetown School of Medicine, gave an introductory talk that pointed to how the old biomedical model is not adequate. The concept of patient compliance with the doctor is destructive. He suggested it be replaced with the concept of partnership between doctor and patient.

Meanwhile, the Office of Alternative Medicine began to take additional actions to lessen the apparent monopoly of allopathic medicine.

Major medical insurance plans began to accept certain alternative medical approaches. Homeopathy became reimbursable through Medicare and other insurance plans. Hospitals have become more patient-minded and some, like the huge Queens Medical Center in Honolulu, have begun to incorporate alternative approaches as well as give patients more say in their own treatment.

There is the same kind of excitement about all of this as there was about the sudden destruction of the Berlin Wall, the unification of Germany, and the fall of the USSR.

It is obvious there has been something at work that transcends the powers of the military and the state and instead follows the will of the people, the mindset of humankind, the consciousness of humanity.

Alternative medicine—an approach to health willed by the people—has changed from slow track to fast track, from skeptical health care professionals to cooperative ones, and from ignorance to sufficient knowledge to make efficient choices.

An army of angels must be breathing a sigh of relief.

But don't expect an army of Good Samaritans to be working for you when you enter Fairyland City's Universal Trade Center. One will do the trick.

Jeremy wanted to help cure his cousin of painful bursitis. Jeremy was in New York. His cousin was in Los Angeles. Jeremy knew that his cousin's insecurity had caused the bursitis and a change in consciousness was needed, so he wrote his own prescription: A visit to the Universal Trade Center. There he would trade his knowledge about the bursitis for relief for his cousin.

Inside, he went into an open cubicle. Activating his controlled daydreaming, he called for an angel. Instantly, a graceful angel appeared in angelic elegance. His controlled daydreaming then went through these stages, each taking only an instant:

A. Gratitude for the angelic response.
B. Identification of the cousin by name, sex, address, and age.
C. Identification of the bursitis problem and its probable cause.

D. A view of his cousin holding his shoulder as the angel hovered by.

E. A sudden movement by the angel that appeared to send something away.

F. A dropping of his cousin's hand from the painful shoulder.

G. His cousin moving the formerly pained shoulder and smiling as he found it free of pain.

Note that daydreaming steps C through G are special for the health problem involved. A different health problem would still entail its identification (C), its major symptom (D), an action by the healing angel (E), an indication of improvement in the condition (F), and finally a picture of normality returned (G).

In the Action Plan that follows, these steps A through G will be specified, knowing that you will refer back to these seven steps with adjustments in steps C–G to fit the abnormality involved.

Here is the procedure to help heal another person at a distance. Before beginning, analyze your motive. If you are doing this magnanimous deed to receive something in return, you may be off on the wrong foot. Success is more likely if you are helping the person to heal for healing's sake.

ACTION PLAN

for Distant Healing

1. Relax.
2. Daydream.
3. With the doorway to Fairyland City enveloped in your bright white light, walk in.
4. Go to the garden and get your key from the drop of water in one of the roses that reflects all the colors.
5. Proceed to the Universal Trade Center.
6. Stand out front and contemplate the healing power of universal life energy.
7. Go into the Universal Trade Center and enter a private open cubicle.
8. Ask for an angel. Wait until one appears in your controlled daydreaming.
9. Do steps A to G as outlined on pages 122–123, adapting C to G to reflect the abnormality involved.
10. Thank the angel. Leave the building.
11. Return to the garden, leaving your key with one of the roses.
12. Pass through the doorway, leaving it open and mentally affirming, "My consciousness is one with universal consciousness. Universal life energy surges through me as I go forth."
13. Open your eyes, feeling great. Visualize your request being met. Know that your request will be met.

THE CRITICAL FACTOR OF YOUR LIFE THAT IS SECOND ONLY TO HEALTH

The Universal Trade Center has another important activity that comes in close second to your helping somebody to heal. It is this: helping you to carry out your goal in life.

Many people trade their soul to the devil. This may sound like the turn of a phrase, but when somebody puts aside a principle to attain great monetary wealth, or to acquire power, or to satisfy lust, they are aborting their goal in life and trading their Creator's purpose for them for a selfish and usually sensory purpose.

If you feel you are leading a life that is off track, if you feel you have lost your way, or if you feel you have been diverted from your path by family or friends who have influenced you, then you are not being true to your soul. Instead, you are living another's life, not your own.

Try as you may, you are in between a rock and a hard place. A change is put off until tomorrow, and tomorrow never comes.

Gary worked for his father-in-law. He did not like the real estate business, but his wife felt more secure, his in-laws were insistent, and whenever he talked about other possible opportunities, they abruptly changed the subject.

After eleven years, three children, and a desultory relationship with his wife and family, Gary suddenly awoke with a cancerous stomach tumor. He knew deep inside that it was an inside problem—inside his very soul. He had two operations. The first separated the tumor from his stomach. The second separated him from his wife.

He flew to a city over a thousand miles away, far enough from his wife and her family, but not too far as to prevent him from seeing his children. Within a week he got a job as a market researcher for a project builder. A year later, he was offered a lucrative arrangement with the marketing arm of a refrigeration company. He knew it was right for him. He felt creative in his work.

He sent for his separated wife and children. They rejoined him. Once again, he felt he was captain of his soul.

This tale of fifteen years could have been shortened to a fraction of that wasted length with the help of controlled daydreaming and a fairy godmother or guardian angel. Both are waiting for you at the Universal Trade Center. With their help, you can trade an old life for a new life.

> If you are barely subsisting . . .
>
> If you are working from 9 to 5, 9 to 5,
> and 9 to 5 . . .
>
> If you are bored and know there is more to life
> than the life you are living . . .
>
> If you are stuck in a rut . . .
>
> If you are ready for a major change in your life . . .

Then you are ready for a visit to the Universal Trade Center.

Yes, you can trade a useless life for a more useful one.

FIND YOUR TRUE PURPOSE IN LIFE

I was a teenager in college when my father died, leaving a raw fur business to be liquidated or run. My family felt that the forty-year-old business had built up such a good name among fur trappers throughout the country that it should not be closed. I was elected to keep it going.

Weekend trips between Cambridge, Massachusetts, and the New York City fur business sufficed to keep things going until I graduated from MIT. From then on, I lived and breathed muskrat pelts, skunk and opossum skins, the long-haired furs of foxes and raccoons and the more stylish mink.

I hated every day. I was outsmarted by suppliers and customers alike. I had to travel to cold country areas and grade the pelts in freezing barns. My purchases were so slow selling that the bank was constantly notifying me to make up overdrafts. In short, I was not living the life I felt was mine. That was my daily prayer.

Enter a guardian angel, I'm sure. The business was closed down by creditors. My brother-in-law, an architect, invited me to do publicity for his firm. My first week resulted in four published news stories about his work. Since architects were not permitted to advertise, I wrote books about his house designs and they were published by major publishers, much to his advantage and, in the process, launching me in my true purpose in life.

Within ten years, I had evolved from how-to books to better your home, to how-to books to better your body, to how-to books to better your mind, and had managed to write fifty books that eventually reached and helped a million people that first decade.

I wish I knew enough in those days to give my guardian angel credit for pointing me in the right direction. I pause to do so now. . . .

Fairyland City is your connection to your guardian angel. You can understand this better if you accept yourself, not as being your body, but as being your consciousness. Then, when you accept the postulate of modern science that there is consciousness behind the order, intelligence, and purpose apparent in the universe, you are ready to perceive your own consciousness as part of this cosmic consciousness.

This is, in my opinion, the greatest step that anybody can take in his or her life.

It opens you up to the greatest luck, the most astounding miracles, and a continuously flowing stream of love, power, and good fortune.

It is as if this cosmic consciousness has been waiting for you. "What took you so long? I thought you would never recognize me. Welcome to invisible support and limitless opportunity."

Something inside you is also jubilant at the union, or reunion. Things happen. I have seen an actor suddenly land a leading role, a struggling accountant find himself made vice president of a large firm, a widow become social hostess of a major hotel.

Whenever a person decides to trade his or her separate consciousness for a joining with universal consciousness, miracles begin to happen. A good place to do this is in the Universal Trade Center.

"UNIVERSAL CONSCIOUSNESS: YOUR WILL BE DONE FOR ME"

At one end of the huge vaulted interior of the Universal Trade Center is an area where the roof ends and you are open to the sky. This is where your controlled daydreaming must take you in order to "get your soul back from the devil."

This expression is again used as a definitive description of what you have done by letting yourself be "lived" by family, friends, or circumstances. The next Action Plan will start the wheels turning to free you from this imprisonment and point you in the direction of your original life mission.

Even though you will daydream in this Action Plan through the "skylight" in the Universal Trade Center, your connection to cosmic consciousness is within you, where your controlled daydreaming takes place.

Each Action Plan in the past has spelled out the steps to enter Fairyland City and then, when the action there is completed, the steps to leave Fairyland City. We will assume you now know these steps, or that you can refer back to previous Action Plans for these beginning and ending steps. We will merely say, "Enter Fairyland City" at the start, and "Leave Fairyland City" at the close.

Before doing this Action Plan, review the pros and cons of your life's activities at present. Ask deep, meaningful questions that revolve around the target question: Should I trade this life for one more suitable to me?

The answer will come. If it is "Yes," you are ready to do this Action Plan.

ACTION PLAN

to Free Yourself to Live Your Own Life

1. Enter Fairyland City.

2. Go to the Universal Trade Center, enter it, and stand at the far left open-to-the-sky area.

3. Imagine that the light above you is really a reflection of the light within you.

4. Turn this imagined concept into the realization that it is true. See a vast and brilliant light within you.

5. This light within you embraces you like a member of the opposite sex. It is like the brilliance of a great person you yearn to be near.

6. Mentally state, "I want the freedom to be one with this brilliant light."

7. A great feeling of love comes over you—love for your own true self.

8. You remain immersed in this love for several ecstatic moments.

9. You exit, watching for an angel, fairy godmother, or genie, and thanking this manifestation of cosmic help as you leave.

10. Leave Fairyland City.

There is now a miraculous link between you and the universe. When you decide to link your consciousness with universal consciousness by doing this Action Plan, miracles begin to happen.

It does not matter whether you are an influential person or a relative nobody, rich or poor, young or old, man or woman. You begin to make the right decisions automatically. You begin to want only the things you really need. You begin to move your life in the direction that fits your unique capabilities.

You begin to enjoy a fairy-tale life.

THE WIZARD THAT SHOWS UP REGULARLY

Deep down inside all of us is the knowledge that we are more than we appear to be and that there is more to life than meets the eye.

This is evident in the prevalence of myths and sagas that last through the ages, of religion itself, of fairy tales, and even of the boogie man that succeeds in terrorizing every child.

But, on the South Island of New Zealand, in the picturesque town of Christchurch, a person shows up in the town square who calls himself the Wizard. He is a long-time resident of the town who has adopted the role of town wizard as a fulfillment of his own life.

Crowds await his scheduled appearances and you can hear a leaf drop as he makes his pronouncements about events of Christchurch and beyond. He once made a wrong prediction about a local soccer game result and resigned in disgrace. But the roar of protest quickly brought him back to his regular town square schedule.

People of all classes and credos consult him on their problems—health, relationships, finances. His popularity has grown through the years because of his valuable advice.

Is this man an impostor? Is the self-adopted title of Wizard a fraud? Are the people of Christchurch being bamboozled?

The answer to all three questions may have been, at the start, yes, yes, and yes.

But, something has happened since then. The deep-down feeling inside the New Zealanders that wizardry is indeed possible and that this man may indeed be a wizard has imbued this once-impostor with an expanded consciousness. His right brain hemisphere has become more active, joining with a higher intelligence. He will eventually attain a cosmic consciousness as crowds attune their consciousness to his and support his pronouncements.

You may one day be buying a plane ticket to south New Zealand to experience an even more exalted Wizard of Christchurch.

What does this tell us about ourselves? Pause a moment and think about it.

Are we not all potential wizards? If so, why don't we all begin to manifest wizardry in our lives?

Geniuses are not all born. Many of them are made. They are unmade, too. Many a genius burns brightly as a young child and is extinguished before third grade, put down by exasperated teachers who douse the fire. So do low marks that do not give originality its proper credit. So do disciplinary measures that degrade, uncomplimentary remarks that lower self-esteem, and reduced teacher awareness of special talent.

Even if we emerge from the equalizing educational process as valedictorian of our class, the brutality of the material world can quickly level us off.

Fortunately for humankind, the opposite is also true. The factors that move us up are within us. If we look within and recognize we are still in touch with our Creator, we behave more spiritually. Other people respond to our wisdom. As more people support us, we grow in consciousness.

Welcome, Wizard of your town.

HOW TO TRADE AN UNHAPPY RELATIONSHIP FOR A HAPPIER ONE

Love is the greatest power in the universe. It can drive men and women to commit the most heinous crimes. Or it can lift them to the highest peaks of ecstasy.

Charms and incantations have been used by people all over the world to help them reach their romantic goals.

In Haiti, a hotbed for black magic, anything from snakeskins to excrement is used to augment the spoken spell.

These objects and rituals help to focus and reinforce the imagined picture of the person's desired result. They add energy to that person's consciousness. The knowledge science is acquiring about the energy of consciousness is beginning to throw some light on why love potions and magical incantations do the job. Consciousness is a creative power.

Whenever consciousness is used for evil or to control a person against that person's will, it is called black magic. It may work temporarily, but then there is usually a backlash and the deed is undone, or it is done again to the doer.

Whenever consciousness is used for good or to assist another person, it works permanently and instead of a backlash, there is a reward in kind by the universe.

The universe is, of course, in favor of happy relationships based on total love. If relationships deteriorate, humanity's law may say "hold fast," but universal law seems to be in favor of finding a new relationship for each of the parties, providing neither of the parties is hurt by such a change.

We are not advocating the breaking of either codes of law—nature's or humanity's. We are merely pointing out the courses available and the choices that are each person's job to make.

The Bible says, "In the beginning was the Word." Nearly a century ago, Charles W. Littlefield, M.D., decided to research the creative power of the word. He made supersaturated solutions of mineral salts. Then, by imaging crystal forms, these exact forms began to manifest. Watching through a microscope, he saw matter become the obedient servant of his mind with "exactness that must be due to some marvelous law we do not understand."

The Word, it appears, can be a spoken word or a mental image. We are getting closer to understanding why the words we speak and the images we hold in our mind are creative forces that tend to produce "in kind."

"I can't go out with you tonight," a young man told a girl he was trying to break off with. "My grandmother died." Three days later, his fib came true.

Transcendental Meditation is the use of mantras, or holy words. Repeated again and again, they elevate the consciousness. You know that is their purpose, so they work whether you know their meaning or not.

Is this not like a placebo given to you by your doctor? You do not know that really it is a sugar pill, but you are told it will cure you, and because you believe the doctor, it works.

The ancients often used the placebo effect in the form of pictorial signs and symbols that brought about healing of the body or healing of relationships. These diagrams still do the job they were originally designed to do.

Such a diagram is Solomon's Seal. It has the power to bring two people together. This power goes back thousands of years. This seems like the dim, dim past to us. Really it is but a second in the stream of universal consciousness.

Are you yearning to be with a certain person? Would you like to have that person drawn to your side as if by an unseen power? If you will not be hurting someone in the process, and if you are willing to permit that person to leave if such is his or her will, then Solomon's Seal will help do it.

The Seal is illustrated on page 137. Look at the Seal, but do not try to understand it. Accept it as the pledge of a powerful consciousness millennia ago to bring two people together, but with no promise to keep them together. It may be quite painful to separate, but that is the price that must be paid.

A male lecturer used the Seal to attract a female psychologist to join him on his seminar tours. She closed her practice and traveled with him. But the relationship lasted only three months.

Here is how to use Solomon's Seal.

ACTION PLAN

to Attract a Certain Person to Your Side

1. Trace the Seal onto a piece of white paper.
2. Acquire a photo of the person you wish to attract. In the absence of a photo, make a sketch. Hold the traced seal and photo (or sketch) on your lap.
3. Using the steps provided in previous Action Plans for going to Fairyland City, go to the Universal Trade Center and enter a cubicle.
4. Feel great respect for the power of the Seal.
5. Place Seal and photo (or sketch) together face to face.
6. Leave Fairyland City.

From now on, keep the Seal and picture close to your body wherever you go. Keep it on your seat in the car, under your pillow at night, in your desk at work . . . until the two of you meet.

THE MATERIAL LIMITS OF THE UNIVERSAL TRADE CENTER

Some readers may be waiting for instructions on how to use the Universal Trade Center to trade in their old car for a new one, or to replace their old stereo equipment with more modern equipment, or to look over a collection of stylish new wristwatches to trade their old one in on.

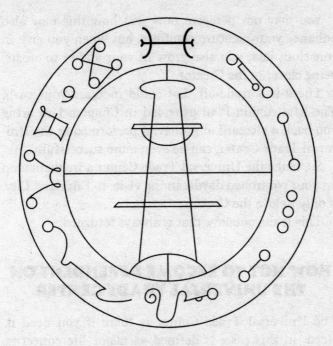

Solomon's Seal

If you are awaiting instructions to trade in your old refrigerator for a new one, you had better make up your mind that other trading centers are a better bet for you.

The Universal Trade Center is based on non-material matters. Life energy, yes. Life goals, yes. Life's partners, yes. But television sets, no. Partners are material, you say. Not exactly. We are our consciousness, not our body. Partners are our soul mates.

If you expected to trade in stocks, bonds, or other securities—sorry. The shares available at the Universal Trade Center are a share in fulfillment, a share in self-realization, and a share in enlightenment.

You may not perceive now just how this may also enhance your creature comforts, but when you give in consciousness, you also grow in your ability to create, being closer to the Creator.

There is a trade-off that could increase your cash. The first Action Plan provided in Chapter 1 to bring you back a blizzard of money, if performed in the Universal Trade Center, can be even more successful.

So, make the Universal Trade Center a frequent stop on your controlled daydreaming visits to Fairyland City, if only to love the Creator.

This is the one love that is always returned.

HOW NOT TO BECOME DEPENDENT ON THE UNIVERSAL TRADE CENTER

The Universal Trade Center is there if you need it. Need, in this case, is defined as major life concerns, largely set forth in this chapter.

These major life concerns may start with minor life misconceptions. One needs to be aware of the possibility of such misconceptions existing, and this awareness needs to be ongoing.

Does one exercise this awareness by reading the editorial pages? By taking continuing education classes? By going to commercial training seminars? Perhaps—with a capital "P."

By far the better way, not eliminating these ways necessarily, but rather adding to them, is to go to the controlled daydreaming state daily by which you enter Fairyland City.

Relax and picture the doorway or the garden to Fairy-land City and just enjoy the picture for a minute or two.

This acts to bring you closer to the Creator. You have been created as a unique individual. Being closer to the Creator moves you away from unnatural ways and closer to the Creator's way for you.

Anything that you do to become more godlike makes you closer to your unique self.

These can often be simple, everyday things, like:

- Paying a debt that should be paid.
- Taking a position that you know is more enlightened.
- Granting a favor that solves a problem for yourself and others.
- Saying something lovingly that needs to be said.
- Changing from a negative to a positive viewpoint.

Can you see an underlying factor behind these actions? It is control. Exercising control is a sensitive matter. "As you sow, so shall you reap." You must be sure you are not being motivated by selfish interest.

This is called the law of karma. It appears to be a universal law. At least there is no way to evade it. You cannot keep secrets from the universal consciousness as it penetrates our own.

There are no masks that can transform selfish motives into magnanimity. You and I are totally responsible for our actions. Responsible actions in turn lead to a life that is on target for meaningful days, joyous months, and godlike years.

A TROUBLE-FREE LIFE DESPITE
A TROUBLED WORLD

There are conditions in the world today that give one pause. A building is bombed. A plane is sabotaged. A subway is gassed. Millions die in African warfare. Millions more are wounded or killed in local wars for independence, or for new boundaries. The threat of nuclear proliferation is rampant. AIDS remains a growing threat. The use of drugs has the potential to fuel crime on every sidewalk and in every home.

Is it little wonder that suicides are on the increase in many parts of the world? And that many young married couples hesitate to bring children into the world?

We are told that a new civilization is emerging. It is traveling, they say, along the information highway. Alvin and Heidi Toffler, authors of *Future Shock,* write that "Humanity faces a quantum leap forward. It faces the deepest social upheaval and creative restructuring of all time. Without clearly recognizing it, we are engaged in building a remarkable new civilization from the ground up."

We are forced to accept this concept. There is no other that conforms with the concept of creation. It leapfrogs hopelessness and gives us hope.

Undoubtedly, the computer will play a role in this new civilization, but as important as that role is, it will never supplant the thirty-billion-component computer called the human brain. It is inconceivable that a computer can be built that will be able to tap the information in higher intelligence.

Nor can we depend on advances in the telephone. A while back, the telephone instituted 1–800 numbers that still are the source of all types of information. Now there are 1–900 numbers that provide psychic readings, professional advice, and fortune-telling. But it is doubtful that there will ever be 1–1000 numbers that, when you dial them, enable you to hear the voice of God.

The human brain does exactly that.

After you have practiced controlled daydreaming, be it with Fairyland City or without, your ability to imagine solutions to problems accurately becomes genius-like; your ability to create fulfilling human relationships becomes wondrous; and your day-to-day decisions that create for you a trouble-free life appear godlike.

They are!

7

THE SUPREME COURT OF FAIRYLAND CITY

Walk into the United States Supreme Court and you are immediately affected by its grandeur. This imposing appearance is created less by domes and columns than it is by silence. There is a hush in the hearing rooms. Even the halls bustling with people have a stillness about them.

The Supreme Court of Fairyland City is even quieter. When you use your controlled daydreaming to locate it, there it is. But, if you try it enter it like other Fairyland City buildings, it is not there.

The reason for this now-you-see-it-now-you-don't phenomenon is that your case is being heard right now.

Denise was incensed at a major airline. She had saved up a number of flying mile certificates to go to her son's graduation and now, even though she was seeking reservations six months in advance, the quota was filled. She decided to take her complaint to the top executives of the airline. But first, knowing the power of her creative imagination, she daydreamed about what she would say.

As she mentally verbalized her position in her imagination, she may not have realized it but judges were listening. These judges were not like the United States Supreme Court justices. They were higher—so high that they sat in judgment of the United States Supreme Court justices. As they listened to Denise state her case, they ruled in her favor.

As a result, when Denise actually made her call to the airline executives, the answer was cordial and affirmative. "Yes, we can arrange another frequent flyer seat for you. When do you wish to go?"

Decisions of Fairyland City's Supreme Court are not based on the U.S. Constitution, nor do they follow any other country's basic laws. They follow universal law, or what might be called cosmic law.

We are all probably more familiar with these universal laws than we are with the U.S. Constitution. Here are a few.

LAWS THAT FORM THE BASIS OF FAIRYLAND CITY SUPREME COURT DECISIONS

We have all become aware of the law of gravity. We deal with it every minute of our lives. But do we know that it is known as the law of gravity only by humans and that its cosmic name is the law of attraction?

All things attract each other, some in proportion to their respective masses, some in accordance with their energetic polarity, some by the amount of their loving compassion.

Side by side with the law of attraction is the law of balance. And there is the law of vibration.

I studied these laws many decades ago under the wise tutelage of one Jacques Bustanoby, founder of Cosmo-Theology. I know of no reference guide to them existent today. But if you are familiar with one particular cosmic law, it can win you a lot of Supreme Court cases. It is the law of karma. Karma is a Sanskrit word meaning "doing" or "action." The law of karma is the law of action and reaction, of cause and effect.

Right action brings right reaction. Know and conform to this cosmic law and you will have the Supreme Court of Fairyland City backing you.

Occasionally, individuals are inspired to intuitively know these cosmic laws. Hermes, who lived over a millennium ago, was one such sage. Two competing civilizations claimed him as their own. The Greeks called Hermes the messenger of the Gods. The Romans called him Mercury and considered him the father of science.

Both the Greeks and the Romans kept the teachings of Hermes secret, feeling that they were only for the innermost leaders. So tightly kept were these secrets for centuries that we still use the words "hermetically sealed" today.

Sometimes cosmic laws are "received" and given to us by individuals who record them. *The Golden Scripts* by William Dudley Pelley (Fellowship Press, Inc., Noblesville, IN) are quite impressive. Listen:

> The gods whom ye serve are not petty gods;
> they are the arbiters of men's welfare over
> whom I reign.

> No greater gentleness, no greater kindliness,
> no greater consideration existeth in the Cosmos
> than that manifesting between high, high forms
> of spiritual entities.

No, cosmic laws are not written in the sky, nor posted on bulletin boards. They just are. And they are everywhere, governing the manifest universe in a non-manifest way.

Sometimes, they peek at us through writers and speakers and suddenly become practical quotable precepts, like "The more good we find to say about a person, the more good that person becomes," or "Where your work speaks for itself, don't interrupt." And, "If you always tell the truth, you don't have to remember anything."

These lighthearted gems are indirect descendants of cosmic law and are a far cry from the rigid, carved-in-stone Ten Commandments that Moses is said to have been given for humankind's guidance. They are the kinds of precepts on which Fairyland City's Supreme Court bases its decisions.

One wording of cosmic precepts that gives us a sort of blueprint for a life that conforms with cosmic law is the Silva Method philosophy:

> You will continue to strive to take part in constructive and creative activities to make this a better world to live in, so that when we move on, we shall have left behind a better world for those who follow. You will consider the whole of humanity, depending on their ages, as fathers or mothers, brothers or sisters, sons or daughters. You are a superior human being; you have greater understanding, compassion, and patience with others.

So simple. Yet it would solve all of our problems if followed by the Earth's people.

STEPPING DOWN ETERNAL LAWS TO THE TIME CALLED NOW

The Fairyland City Supreme Court is not waiting for you to create a test case in order to get their opinion. It does not take a privileged summer vacation. It does not issue its decisions exclusively on Monday.

It is in constant session. It knows all. If there is one way to get its attention more surely, it is to relax and use controlled daydreaming and do so in Fairyland City.

Controlled daydreaming is right brain thinking. Right brain thinking is spiritual world thinking. Daydream in a controlled way with the purpose of enhancing your "constructive and creative activities to make this a better world to live in," and you rise above earthly resistances and barriers such as distance and time. You take the spiritual world route to your target, be it a person, goal, or solution.

It is called subjective communication, as opposed to objective communication.

The advantage of subjective communication over objective communication—the advantage of a spiritual route—depends on the purpose for which you use it.

The prime purpose is to talk to the Creator and listen for the reply.

When you talk to God objectively, you are said to be praying. When God talks to you, you are said to be schizophrenic.

When you talk to God subjectively, and God replies, it is a closed circuit. It is not only a private matter, but you get help—all the help you need to overcome problems. What kind of problems? Every kind of problem you will ever encounter.

Vern was a kind man. When a woman he knew casually approached him for a favor, he not only listened attentively, he granted the favor. The favor was to endorse a second mortgage she was taking out on her home in the amount of $20,000.

Because she was a woman, she explained to Vern, the bank required a male endorsement of the loan.

Vern had forgotten the whole matter when, six months later, he was reminded of it by the bank. Apparently, his friend was three months behind in her second mortgage payments. They had given her two weeks to make a sizable payment. If she did not, the bank explained, they would be looking to Vern for payment.

It was suddenly an impending disaster. Twenty thousand dollars was impossible for Vern to ever contemplate putting his hands on. That same night, he did his controlled daydreaming to contact Jesus. Vern turned the problem over to higher intelligence as represented by Jesus.

Two weeks later, the bank called again to say that a partial payment had been made, but that Vern should still consider himself on notice. Two months later, they called to say the woman sold the house and paid off the second mortgage. Vern was off the hook.

Perhaps the judges of the Supreme Court of Fairyland City are the Ascended Masters, the Great White Brotherhood, and other exalted beings and that when we use our controlled daydreaming faculties to communicate subjectively with higher intelligence, we are communicating with them.

Whatever is happening, it is happening for the best. And it is happening now.

USING CONTROLLED DAYDREAMING TO COMMUNICATE SUBJECTIVELY FOR DAILY BENEFITS

Controlled daydreaming is our connection to God. By activating the right brain hemisphere, it enables us to communicate with the other side. We are in touch with all of God's helpers, from exalted beings through angels, fairies, and elves and including magicians, gurus, and, at times, even you and me.

God is everywhere, including in all of God's creations. When we communicate through controlled daydreaming, we are talking to a higher mind—the godly aspect. This is true whether our controlled daydreaming is with an angel or a neighbor.

If you talk to your neighbor in your controlled day-dreaming, it is subjective communication. It is at a spiritual level. Now it is a matter of what is right, not who is right.

To survive on planet Earth, humankind must end its left brain monopoly of communication and begin to use both brain hemispheres. Using both brain hemispheres—the right brain hemisphere in particular—establishes a connection with God and permits life on earth to be God-inspired.

All of your work through Fairyland City is spiritually oriented and much of it is subjective communication. But Fairyland City is not the only route available to you to communicate subjectively.

You can sit quietly in your living room, close your eyes, relax and, instead of visualizing the doorway to Fairyland City, visualize whomever you wish to contact. You can then begin to imagine a conversation with that person.

That person can be your runaway child, your "impossible" father-in-law, an errant lover, a stubborn partner, a hard-to-please customer, an unruly pupil, even yourself.

There is a difference in the way you "talk" when using subjective communication. Here is an example of how not to talk subjectively. A child is asleep and a mother wishes to talk subjectively to the child and encourage the child not to wet the bed. The mother is in the living room, eyes closed, visualizing the child. Does she say what she might say personally to the child?

"You lousy brat. You wet your bed again, I'll wipe your face in it."

No way. The right brain connection was broken in the first few words. Spiritual communication requires a loving climate and a sense of oneness. If there is acrimony, forget it. If there is polarity, forget it.

You cannot talk down to anyone. You cannot proclaim your own righteousness even if you are right. You must talk on an equal basis, despite any advantages or disadvantages at either end. You must talk not about who is right, but about what is right for the two of you.

Good relationships thrive on good communications. Objective communication—communication with the left brain—must hurdle disappointments, misunderstandings, and resentments. Subjective communication—communication involving the right brain—rises above these obstacles and through love and oneness with higher intelligence reaches a mutual solution.

Here are a number of situations that, by experience, lend themselves to correction through subjective communication:

- A neighbor's antagonism to your pets is defused.
- A parent's objection to a marriage is removed.
- A client's delay in paying your bill is ended.
- An employee's abusive behavior stops.
- A friend who overindulges agrees to seek help.

These are so diversified that the conclusion is evident: subjective communication works at all times. That's because the other side is on your side. It will help you get a raise or a new job. It will enable you to help a drug user to stay clean. It will help an artist to know what paintings will sell best. It will help anybody to improve their efficiency. It helped me to write this book.

The results of subjective communication properly carried out are so sure, so dramatic, and so universal in application that it is a waste of your time and mine to elaborate further other than to review the step-by-step procedure. So here goes:

ACTION PLAN

to Get Your Message Across Without Speaking a Single Word

1. Relax.
2. Daydream.
3. Visualize the person with whom you wish to communicate subjectively.
4. Feel love for that person. If the relationship is beset with rancor, forgive that person and ask to be forgiven.
5. With a feeling of love prevailing, relate your message. Avoid the polarity of "I am right. You are wrong." Instead, relate what you feel is right for both of you—a mutually acceptable solution.
6. End your daydreaming session.

When we were created, we were given free will by our Creator. Despite all the troubles that often come through the exercise of that personal free will, it is not taken away from us.

So do not think that subjective communication is a way of controlling people. It will not work if it is unilateral. It will not work if it hurts anybody.

Sometimes it works through angels, demi-gods, and Kahunas. But unless these cases are reported, we have no way of knowing whether an angelic appearance was the result of somebody's subjective communication or not.

A couple is driving along at night on a narrow mountain road in Hawaii. The headlights pick up a hitchhiker. They stop. It is a middle-aged woman with red hair. She climbs into the back of the car.

"Where are you going?" she asks.

"To Honolulu," the wife replies. "Are you going there, too?"

"No," replies the woman, "I'll get off down the road a ways."

They drive on. "Do you mind if I smoke?" asks the rider.

"No, go ahead," the husband replies.

She lights up and blows her smoke out the window. Suddenly she says, "Pull up on the right there; that's where I get off."

They stop. She gets out and closes the door. Just then a huge truck comes hurtling out of the dark. It slams by, almost sideswiping their car. Had they been driving, there would surely have been a head-on collision. They looked back at their rider. She was nowhere in sight.

No matter to whom they related this event later, the answer was always the same: That was Pele, goddess of the volcano.

The same day I wrote that story, the following story was related to me by the same lady to whom it happened. She was shopping and began to feel dizzy and unwell. She sat down for a while. Still feeling strange, she decided to go back to the retirement residence where she lived. As she was waiting alone for a bus, a lady in a car stopped.

"Where are you going?" she asked my friend. When she told her, the driver replied, "I'm going there, too; climb in."

On the way, it turns out this lady was visiting a person on the same floor as my friend. She helped my friend right to her door. Later, my friend asked her neighbor about her visitor.

"What visitor?"

"She was dressed in white."

"Nobody visited me."

That's the way angels work. Sometimes without a "by your leave."

Why I learned about this angel a few minutes ago, I cannot fathom. So, I did what I figured was expected of me. I shared it with you. Perhaps they thought this might be good public relations.

CASES YOU CAN TURN OVER TO FAIRYLAND CITY'S SUPREME COURT

Forgiveness is a necessity for our survival. It clears our mental air and relieves our stressed body.

This makes it appear to be selfish. But that is an illusion. Actually, the one we forgive benefits, too. Though the act of forgiving is subjective, the relief is mutual.

Forgiveness is often difficult because if there has been an injustice done, we don't want to be guilty of furthering injustice by suspending justice through whitewashing it via forgiveness.

What is seldom realized is that eventually justice is always done. And it is done without our having to sit in judgment. It is done by the highest of Supreme Courts, by the very intelligence that fills all space.

The symbol of this highest of all Supreme Courts is Fairyland City's Supreme Court. It does not have to hear your case, because it already knows more about it than you do. It has already made its decision and has even initiated corrective action.

What, then, is the purpose of visiting Fairyland City's Supreme Court?

There is a strong and valid purpose: to support it.

You support it by visiting it and expressing your love and appreciation for its good works.

"Why me?" you ask. "I am but a piece of dust in the vast cosmos."

That you are. But every piece of dust is a piece of God.

Remember the new Einsteinian paradigm that has replaced the old Newtonian concept that says all natural laws are fixed? Forget it. That's out the quantum physics window. Now we know that consciousness creates those natural laws and can also re-create them.

So support of the Universal Supreme Court by your consciousness in effect continues a good thing.

All you need to do is enter Fairyland City. Daydream about its Supreme Court. Applaud its work mentally.

By so doing, you turn over all of your disputes to that Court.

And justice is done.

BAILIFFS OF THIS COURT AT WORK

If one assumes that the justice meted out at a cosmic level can be channeled through ordinary people as well as through fairies, angels, and gurus, then the Supreme Court has many bailiffs working for it.

The blind Helen Keller, Mother Theresa, and Father Damian are examples of these earthbound angels. But not all of them are such standouts. Some of these special people work at a more subtle level.

Take the noted lyricist, Oscar Hammerstein II. He lived from 1895 to 1960 and teamed up with Jerome Kern, a musician, to write the most inspiring songs of the century. He gave joy and hope to millions of his day and will continue to strengthen generations far into the future.

Two aspects to his work alert me to his special bailiffship: he filled his lyrics with daydreams, and his lyrics were bursting with positive thinking.

Here are some examples of his lyrical daydreams that remind listeners of this important mental activity:

"When I grow too old to dream, I'll have you to remember."

And from *The King and I,* "I have dreamed that your arms are lovely."

From *It Might As Well Be Spring,* we hear, "I'm as busy as a spider spinning daydreams."

"If you don't have a dream, how you gonna have a dream come true?" This is from *Happy Talk.*

His lines that express positive thinking inspire listeners to never, never quit. An example that also includes the dream theme is from *Climb Ev'ry Mountain.* It exhorts you to "Follow ev'ry rainbow, till you find your dream."

Can you feel your blood tingle as you read these?

"When you walk through a storm, hold your head up high and don't be afraid of the dark."

"You may be as brave as you make believe you are."

"Walk on, walk on, with hope in your heart, and you'll never walk alone."

Oscar Hammerstein II did not have an easy life while he was making a name for himself. Undoubtedly, he had help from the other side when he wrote such "martial music" words as, "Walk on through the wind, walk on through the rain, though your dreams be tossed and blown."

He kept dreaming of new hits. Those daydreams brought him new poetry, which he put on paper. Years later, they were put to music and inspired millions.

Speaking about the purpose of life, Oscar Hammerstein II said, "I don't know why I was born, beyond the fact that I know why everybody was born. Everybody was born to advance the life in this universe, the life that we all live."

All the institutions of Fairyland City work through people. They work through angels, they work through ascended masters, they work through all the creatures of the Creator. And that includes you and me.

We are among its bailiffs.

A BROADER VIEW OF THE COURT'S CALENDAR

An abused wife decides to take her husband to court. She sues in a local court. To the extent that the local court is headed by a dedicated judge, her case is also being heard by Fairyland City's Supreme Court.

You do not have to research the validity of this fact in the dusty tomes of jurisprudence. It is a matter of simple logic: If consciousness is a oneness, then justice is supported by all consciousness, all intelligence, wherever it is.

Only humans who feel separate are separate. That's why the word "dedicated" is applied to the local judge. A judge who is not dedicated to justice is a separated judge.

If you appear before a dedicated local judge to defend yourself against a wrongful citation for speeding, you can count on support from the Fairyland City Supreme Court.

Likewise, if you sue to collect a legitimate debt, to enforce a fair contract, or to recover medical costs incurred, even though you are in a local court, your case is considered of universal importance. You do not even have to know about the Fairyland City Supreme Court. You still have its support, automatically.

While the Supreme Court justices are supporting thousands of dedicated judges in their quests for righteousness for all, they are also looking at the big pictures.

Big pictures are the larger world situations that involve resolution in the direction of justice for all. So, these Supreme Court Justices . . .

- see world leaders arriving in a huge stadium shaking hands, embracing, and going about their work in the world arena in total harmony.
- see the White House and send the president and his staff strength, wisdom, and understanding.

- see the leaders of two countries who may be in a confrontation meeting, shaking hands, and arriving at mutual accord.

- see a particular political figure who appears to be mistaken or misled bathed in the light of enlightenment.

- see the planet Earth bathed in the light of material respect and love.

Why not hold some of these pictures in your mind to support the Supreme Court judges of Fairyland City?

You will be using your controlled daydreaming in an especially creative way—concretely making this a better world to live in.

DO THE SUPREME COURT JUSTICES HAVE A SENSE OF HUMOR?

There is an apparent heaviness in reading about Supreme Court proceedings. The laws of man are complex and the history of their enforcement, researched to find past precedents for present use, can be a maze of frustration.

The decisions that follow can mean life or death, family unity or family division, riches or deprivation. Yet when acting at the highest level, those who mete out an overriding justice in the world can exhibit a lightness that defies the standard images of the robed or wigged justices.

Seldom is this humor a rib-cracking, belly-laughing affair, but more commonly it is a sardonic type of humor often expressed as "coincidence" or "synchronicity."

Lincoln and Kennedy were both assassinated. Nothing funny about that. But look at what higher intelligence has done with this scenario:

> There are seven letters in each name. Both
> presidents had legality of election contested.
> Both were directly concerned with the issue
> of civil rights. Both were slain on Friday and
> in the presence of their wives.

> Lincoln was elected in 1860. Kennedy was elected
> in 1960. Their successors were named Johnson
> and were Southern Democrats who previously
> served in the U.S. Senate.

> Andrew Johnson was born in 1808. Lyndon
> Johnson was born in 1908. Booth and Oswald
> were murdered before their trials could be
> arraigned. Booth and Oswald were Southerners
> favoring unpopular ideas. Lincoln's secretary,
> named Kennedy, advised him not to go to the
> theater. Kennedy's secretary, named Lincoln,
> advised him not to go to Dallas. John Wilkes
> Booth and Lee Harvey Oswald each contain
> fifteen letters.

> Andrew Johnson and Lyndon Johnson each
> contain thirteen letters.

> Lincoln and Kennedy were carried on the
> same caisson.

Booth and Oswald received quick justice. But the rest of us are left scratching our heads and wondering what the hidden message is. Perhaps one day, we'll know.

What did Edison do in the process of giving everybody's voice an increased range to merit losing his own hearing?

What did Ludwig von Beethoven do in his private life to be the brunt of such sardonic humor as, after creating such exquisite sounds for the world to enjoy, to lose his own hearing?

Today, walking together to lunch, I asked my wife if she could recall from her knowledge of history such comparable and sadly humorous events. As we were eating, a person from the office said the bookkeeper wanted to see us.

"I wonder why?" I asked my wife. "I paid the bill. Maybe I didn't sign the check."

"Or it could have something to do with guest dinner charges," my wife offered.

I continued to think of other financial reasons why the bookkeeper wanted to see us. Lunch finished, we went to the office and knocked on the bookkeeper's door. When she saw us, she picked up a book.

"The director asked me to return with thanks this book you lent her."

The bookkeeper returned a book with thanks for the favor we had done for somebody else. Were the powers-that-be expressing a sense of humor? And was it in response to our search for such examples?

THE POWER OF BELIEVING IN SPIRITUAL LAW

If I have not already told you, public relations is my basic profession. And one of my best clients is God.

A California woman has been in touch with me over the years regarding the alleged misuse of a family trust. The financial stress it was meting out to her made her think of nothing else. Soon it was her health that became our main topic of concern.

Finally, I convinced her that her health was being affected by her constant worrying about the trust and its attendant lawsuits.

"What do I do now?" she asked.

"Turn it over to God," I replied.

"To whom?" she asked, taken totally by surprise.

"Let go and let God," I repeated.

"How do I do that?" she asked, somewhat stunned.

"Program yourself that whenever you start to think about the trust matter, you instead think of God." I reminded her of how to relax and give herself that instruction. She seemed doubtful, but agreed.

She phoned me a few days later. A new approach appeared out of the blue. To me, it seemed a beginning of divine help, and to her, it seemed a total miracle. She would continue to program herself, she promised. And her health had already started to improve.

The laws of the cosmos are powerful laws. They are often in direct opposition to humanity's laws. Collisions between the two usually result in a higher justice being done, even though humanity's laws appear to prevail.

Refugee after refugee from Communist East Germany was shot to death trying to escape via the Berlin Wall. Then, suddenly, the Berlin Wall is down and their entire families, who could not join them in their fatal attempt at freedom, are themselves free.

It is not easy for us to believe in spiritual law. If one is more evident and overpowering than the other, is not the material world's laws—enacted, codified, and enforced by humankind—the more real?

We learn from the mistakes of others because we do not live long enough to make them ourselves.

We are told that necessity is the mother of invention, but more frequently find that it is frustration that is the father of success.

Money is our material world god. Just about everything we do in life is to make money or to spend it. It is said that money is the root of all evil, but isn't the root of all evil the lack of money? Such a lack leads to the fracture of humanity's laws left and right, from shoplifting to robbery.

Just when we think we can make both ends meet, somebody moves the ends. Finally, we find that the only way to double our money is to fold it in half and keep it in our purse or pocket.

At the end of life, as we begin to face the reality of the spiritual world, money is still predominant in our thoughts. We can't take it with us. Understood. But how do we make it last until we're ready to go?

Let's shift gears from material to spiritual law.

Now money is common property. It belongs to all. It flows through you as you make it and spend it, a symbol of the energy you put out and get back.

Samoans learn that everything belongs to everybody. They live a happy life of true freedom. Then they move to the United States. Soon many are in prison. In Hawaii's prisons there are usually more Samoans than any other nationality, unlearning Samoa's more spiritual laws.

When we understand and apply spiritual principles, we need to keep our eye on material world principles, even if only from the point of view of that old adage "When in Rome, do as the Romans do."

One of the great spiritual leaders, who is the source of much of our wisdom about spiritual law, is Jesus. It is less in the teachings of the Christian religions, which are largely about his life, than it is in the words as quoted in the New Testament and his deeds.

He was so much the perfect expression of the infinite consciousness that he never considered the physical body the real one. He saw beyond it to its spiritual idea as conceived by God.

To believe in spiritual law actively is to eliminate material misconceptions that are not godlike. The body is one such misconception. We consider it full of imperfections and potential problems and, because the mind creates the body, it begins to develop imperfections and problems.

Because Jesus was himself the perfect expression of the spiritual, he enabled the perfect being to come into manifestation by his mere presence.

So he was a healer. He could clearly perceive perfect wholeness in a human being and instantly wipe from the patient's mind, as well as his own, all that appeared as disease. The patient's body followed suit.

He did not need medical techniques. They followed material law. His spiritual law was so much more powerful. Even when he visited the lepers, he had no thought of becoming infected himself. He healed with God's power flowing through him.

If you can know the perfect life force and infinite energy flowing through yourself and others, as did Jesus, you too could be a healer. You would simply reach out toward that life force, revitalizing and re-energizing it, and perfect health would instantly be made manifest.

HOW TO INTENSIFY YOUR OWN SPIRITUAL POWER

A number of success purveyors advocate adopting the practice of hanging around successful people. The logic behind this is based on the theory that you begin to imitate the people around you.

Were you to hang around spiritual people, the same could possibly be true. But whereas people successful in the material world take material world actions that observers can emulate, spiritual people are spiritual by dint of their thoughts which, because they cannot be seen, are not easy to copy.

To intensify your own spiritual power, here are simple and productive steps to take.

Simple Steps to Spiritual Power

A. Relax and daydream about theater, music, and art.

B. Relax and daydream about folklore and legend, less about evil stepmothers and wicked fairies and more about heroes, idols, religious symbols, and rituals.

C. Relax and be quiet with a consciousness of the cosmos. Feel love.

D. Relax and be quiet in the garden of Fairyland City. Feel love.

E. Relax and be quiet in any building of Fairyland City. Feel love.

F. Relax and attune your consciousness to the consciousness of the cosmos. Feel love.

We are all at different levels of enlightenment. To try to jump ahead too fast will only spin our wheels.

The best procedure is to start with A. If bored, move immediately to B, et cetera, until you feel that you are not challenged by the stage you are in. Stay in that stage, be it C or D or E, moving on only when you feel you are hungry for more.

The stage you arrive at is hard to describe. Your body remains healthy. You enjoy the normal and orderly process of life. Abundance flows through you. Relationships are smooth and rewarding. The ship of life sails along on smooth seas.

When eventually you are ready to retire and you look back, you see you have prepared a better life for those who follow.

8

THE GENIUS AVAILABLE TO YOU FROM THE HOUSE OF WISDOM

The difference between animals and humans lies primarily in consciousness. Animals function instinctively and automatically, without conscious decision. They are largely controlled by their genes. Humans have conscious awareness. They are connected to their spiritual source and function intelligently.

However, many humans have disconnected themselves from their spiritual source. Their consciousness is monopolized by the physical world to the exclusion of their spiritual identity.

This limits their intelligence. They make mistakes. In fact, you might say they make one mistake after another, repeating them over and over. Even though each mistake causes suffering, mental or physical or both, they are prone to repeat them.

Here are some of the mistakes that spiritually disconnected people keep making.

- They attack, maim, and murder each other.
- They make war on each other in the name of the Creator.
- They cheat and lie in order to get control over others.
- They abuse one another, distrust one another, and take from one another.
- They covet each other's mates and property.
- They use alcohol and drugs to escape from their emptiness.
- They poison the environment and exploit our natural resources.
- They shoplift, steal, and rob.

As a result of these mistakes, such people appear to have a limited intelligence. They lead a life marred by unwanted conditions, wrong decisions, unpredictable people, and—worst of all—nerve-wracking, body-destroying stress.

Humans who continue to recognize their spiritual nature lead an entirely different life. That is because they not only have a visible means of support, but they recognize their connection to their Creator and so they are in turn recognized by their Creator.

They make the right decisions. They are motivated in the right directions. They meet the right people. They are lucky. They are in the right places at the right time. They have meaningful dreams that they are able to learn from. They can ask for help and get flashes of insight. Their guessing ability is uncanny.

You are such a person. You know how to relax and daydream in a controlled way. In other words, you know how to contact your spiritual source.

When you are able to contact your spiritual source, you are able to heal yourself and others. You are able to ask for a dream to contain information to solve a particular problem, have such a dream, remember it, and understand it. You are able to improve your relationships through subjective communication. You are able to imagine a sticky situation that you have, ask for a particular end result acceptable to all concerned, imagine it happening, and create it.

Does this sound like you are some kind of genius? You are.

THE HOUSE OF WISDOM HELPS YOU TO MANIFEST YOUR TRUE GENIUS

You have already learned to use the magic facilities of Fairyland City in many ways.

While relaxed and using your controlled daydreaming faculty, you have healed, you have corrected unwanted situations, and you have communicated without speaking a single word.

The House of Wisdom will now take you a quantum leap forward, boosting your IQ, catapulting your intelligence, and imbuing you with breathtaking wisdom.

There are many computer buffs who would like to take a different route and race you to the finish line. Their use of computers has taken giant strides forward, too. Here are some of the mental tasks these so-called fifth generation computers can do:

- They can play such games as backgammon and chess.
- They can diagnose diseases and prescribe treatments.
- They can solve mathematical equations, even advanced calculus.
- They can analyze electrical circuits.
- They can test theorems.

They are still growing in maturity and may soon also be able to:

- Help discover new areas to mine.
- Provide limited management administration.
- Acquire new abilities through simulation.

But will they ever be able to match their creator's intelligence? Just as humans will never be able to match God's, computers will never be able to match humans.

Twenty years ago, I was in Tokyo on one of many visits. At that time I had dinner with a Japanese computer engineer who was working at one of the few government-subsidized laboratories. He explained that his project at that time was to develop a computer that, instead of running on electrical energy, ran on psychotronic energy—the energy of consciousness.

This computer, if ever created, could possibly become a cosmic computer, tapping in on superconsciousness and providing original ideas, unique solutions, and even what we call wisdom.

The American Heritage Dictionary defines wisdom as the "understanding of what is true, right, or lasting."

Does this satisfy you? Frankly, it leaves me with a great loneliness. But, let's read further; maybe some of the later definitions will be more satisfying: common sense, sagacity, good judgment, learning, erudition.

Common sense is further defined as native good judgment. We know neither is wisdom in its highest sense. Learning is thrown back to wisdom in its definition. Sagacity is called keen intelligence. Erudition is thrown back to learning. So it all adds up to a dead-end street.

If we were to try to define wisdom as we understand it, we would not give it a static look. We would make it dynamic, because we appreciate wisdom's dynamic mode. It moves in a splendid direction. It can lead to peace, love, consensus, and success.

The International Dictionary comes closer to this: "knowledge of what is true or right, coupled with just judgment as to action."

Now we are getting somewhere. Action becomes part of wisdom, which is as it should be. Action is the key to the wisdom generated at the House of Wisdom.

Don't expect from the House of Wisdom such cute gems as "If you always tell the truth, you don't have to remember anything." Or "Good thoughts bear good fruit." Or "Blessed are those who can give without remembering and take without forgetting." This is wisdom, but not for the House of Wisdom.

Here are the kinds of action questions involving wisdom that are the specialty of the House of Wisdom:

"I signed a contract when I sold my business, preventing me from going into the same business for five years. Three years are over. Can I restart it now?"

"Everything points to that site being the best for our company's expansion. Should we buy it?"

"My live-in boyfriend thinks the arrangement is permanent. I want marriage and children. There is another prospect. Should I make the change?"

The answers to these questions require wisdom. Learning would be the hard way. Common sense does not reach far enough. Sagacity and erudition might get you to first base, but no further. But the House of Wisdom can enable you to make a home run.

As to the computer world's information highway, it has its roadblocks. Time is one of them. Techno-boosters are finding it takes time, lots of time, to troll the Internet, search and download masses of data, and sort their e-mail.

This electrical communication takes so much time that it is largely in the hands of those with the most time on their hands, like partly unemployed, thrill-seeking teenaged males and bored retirees. Even if wisdom could by some miracle appear on the electronic screens, it is doubtful if it would be recognized.

There is talk among the so-called cybernauts of virtual community, virtual democracy, even virtual reality. These virtual "experiences" are their avowed goals. Lots of luck, fellows. But, take my word for it, there is no such thing as virtual wisdom.

HOW TO RECOGNIZE
GENUINE WISDOM

"Wise men learn by other men's mistakes, fools by their own."

This proverb has the ring of wisdom, but is it really as sagacious as it sounds?

What it is saying is that you should watch the fellow walking in front of you. If he drops from sight, you know he fell into a manhole and you should walk around it.

"Words may show a man's wit, but actions his meaning."

Wisdom? Or not? My personal opinion is that this is getting closer, but has not quite arrived. One can be fooled by a man's actions as well as his words. True wisdom goes further. If you have true wisdom, you can measure a man without knowing his words or his actions.

"God loves us, not so much for what we are, but for what He can make us."

Proverb for daily living? Or pearl of wisdom? We have arrived at wisdom. Its characteristics are spirituality and growth.

When you put a problem to the intelligence in Fairyland City's House of Wisdom, the solution will have these two characteristics: spirituality and growth. It will radiate measurable dimension that you will find hard to put your finger on—a dimension beyond intelligence.

Genius, brilliance, and eternal greatness are the marks of wisdom, but wisdom goes even further. It can leave you breathless.

What is the path wisdom takes to reach you? Is it a book, a classroom, and a teacher? Is it via a library, an encyclopedia, a page, and a line? Is it via a chance meeting, a conversation, and an event?

These may all be valuable paths, paths by which information, awareness, and guidance can reach you, but these are not the usual paths that wisdom can take.

These are material world paths. Wisdom usually arrives by a spiritual path. Spiritual paths are the domain of the right brain hemisphere, which we activate when we use our imagination and daydream.

Am I saying that true wisdom comes to us only while we are in a meditative, imaginative, or controlled daydreaming state? Basically, yes. That is because the genius within us all is still sleeping. It has been lulled to sleep by the physical world. Turn off the physical world and it awakens.

Nicholas Tesla began experimenting with electricity. This newly discovered phenomena lent itself to some dramatically "shocking" experiments. Tesla, a natural showman himself, would light up a room with almost blinding light. Viewers considered it unbelievable and astounding. Nobody, probably not even Tesla, suspected that electricity would lead to the lighting of cities, the warming of homes, or the advent of radio, television, and computers.

Our ability to tap into higher intelligence for specific wisdom is in the same stage now. We look at it as some dramatic experiment.

You now look at your use of the House of Wisdom as some dramatic experiment. But as you begin to use it with some regularity and success, you begin to acquire the ability to enter the House of Wisdom at will, merely by daydreaming.

You will have trained your mind to tap into the universal source of wisdom. And when you receive it, you will recognize it.

THE RIGHT BRAIN AS A RECEPTOR OF WISDOM

The right brain would never rate very high on an IQ test. But it would enable an executive to beat out all of his or her competitors.

The left brain is adept at solving short-range problems. The right brain sees the whole picture and it goes for long-range, permanent solutions. Wise men and women, prophets, and geniuses have an active right brain hemisphere. They realize they have a mission. They go beyond their personal good and work for the common good.

We are talking about only ten percent of the population. Ninety percent of the people on this planet are left brain thinkers. Take a look at a stadium some afternoon or evening—tier after tier of left brain thinkers. Open up to the legal ads in a daily newspaper. Check out the divorces, bankruptcies, foreclosures, and other lawsuits. Are they people who are connected to higher intelligence—to wisdom—via their right brain hemisphere? And what about the hospitals? Are right-brained people stressed into illness as often as left brained? And who fills the prisons? The enlightened and the wise?

Left-brained people are stand-outs in the wrong way. Right-brained people are much less obvious—and in the right way. They are more constructive and creative. They function selflessly for the common good.

Are you ready to take another step in your right brain development? Are you ready to visit the House of Wisdom?

Warning: It is not a tourist attraction. You go there only with the most serious of intentions—the intention to solve a critical problem.

If you do not have such a problem, continue to visit Fairyland City for the various purposes already discussed, and hold the House of Wisdom for its proper time.

Here are ten examples of critical problems that require wisdom to solve, the kind of spiritual inspiration that comes to you via the House of Wisdom.

- To buy or not to buy. Not paper clips, but buildings, property, patents, companies, et cetera.
- To sell or not to sell.
- To pursue the same path or a different one.
- To marry or not marry; to divorce, or not.
- To travel a chosen route or a different one.
- To go or not to go.
- To invest in this or something else.
- To seek this cure for an illness or a different one.
- To help a particular person or not. If so, how.
- To write on this subject or another one, and the same regarding other creative activities, such as painting, sculpting, composing, et cetera.

When I went to the Massachusetts Institute of Technology (MIT) a half century ago, consciousness did not officially exist. Its existence just was not recognized. No research was done on consciousness.

Later, astronaut Edgar Mitchell got his doctorate at MIT. He became struck with the intelligence that fills all space on his trip to the moon. On his return, he decided to do research on consciousness, but there was no university sponsoring such research, especially MIT, so he formed the Institute of Noetic Sciences.

In the past twenty years, there has probably been no force greater than the Institute in promoting an understanding of the mind's place in the universe.

It has not been a lone effort. The Institute has encouraged research into consciousness—and consequently into your and my sources of wisdom—in a number of universities, foundations, and research institutes. To involve the public in this search, it has teamed up with the Hartley Film Foundation, New Dimensions Radio, and Michael Tom's radio interviews.

It is a long, hard struggle. A left-brain world is not turned into a bicameral brain world in a day, or even a century.

The author's approach to you via angels and fairies is a desperate attempt to bypass your own inevitable left-brain bias and to show you the way to lead a more ideal life, expressing your Creator's wish for you.

Consciousness is still but a frontier of science even today. It is less known and understood than the far reaches of outer space. This speaks volumes about how you have been intimidated by the material world institutions.

As scientists probe the depths of the atom, they are beginning to see intelligence at work. Some of the bolder scientists are extrapolating hypotheses that all space is filled with conscious intelligence. But they are not blasting this too loudly, because the grants they receive for this research are controlled by left-brain people. Why risk their livelihood so you can live a better life?

But, cheer up. All is not lost. The showdown is at hand. You are about to contact the source of wisdom directly.

HOUSE OF WISDOM ACTION PLAN

You may not have a reason to visit the House of Wisdom now, but no life is without its turning points. These times of critical decisions are when such a visit becomes advisable so that the highest wisdom guides you.

Examples of critical decision times are given earlier in this chapter, but these are merely to give you a fix on their importance. There is no way that all the possible crises that can face you can be covered. Actually, the list is endless.

So wait for the time of need for your visit to the House of Wisdom. But meanwhile, here are the instructions for receiving the wisdom that will see you through.

ACTION PLAN

for Receiving Wisdom to Make an Important Decision

1. Enter Fairyland City.
2. Go to the House of Wisdom, identifiable by a large shell antenna on the center of the roof.
3. As you enter, feel love for the divine source of wisdom.
4. Go to the center and bow your head.
5. Mentally state your problem verbally, daydreaming about it as you go.
6. When you finish, begin thinking about the solution.
7. The first solution that comes to you is from the divine source of wisdom. It feels as though you are making up that solution. That is the correct feeling.
8. Thank the divine source of wisdom.
9. Leave Fairyland City.

Begin to implement the solution you have received as soon as is feasible. It is a solution given to you for now. Waiting could invite changes that would likely entail a different solution.

Do not have doubts about yourself. This tapping of spiritual sources for help is something that you have practiced for a period of time sufficient enough to make you a skilled daydreamer. You relax physically. You quiet the mind. You picture realistically. You desire, believe, and expect. Trust the solution you have received. Implement it skillfully.

HAVE YOU A RIGHT TO TAP INTO THIS WISDOM?

When a person solves a difficult problem by tapping divine wisdom, there is frequently a feeling of having robbed a safe, or intruded into some sacrosanct chambers.

I am quick to assure such a person that he or she had every right to be in a productive daydream that yielded an inspired solution.

In fact, not just a right, but a duty.

We have let the material world pull us away from our spiritual birthplace. We have become separated from our source. I like that bumper sticker that reads, "If you feel separated from God, you know who moved."

I have listed the many types of mistakes that people make as a result of their left-brained thinking. Our planet is on the verge of destruction as a result.

What you do when you go to the House of Wisdom for answers, or for that matter anywhere in Fairyland City, is begin to connect the Creator to creation once again.

Major changes and improvements must take place on Earth as more and more people do this.

Let me now go to the House of Wisdom and ask what some of these changes might be . . . .

- People will become more responsive to their spiritual nature and less to their animal nature.

- People will be able to intuit the future and head off problems.

- Prisons will gradually empty as crime, violence, and substance abuse lessen.
- Labor and management will realize that they share the same goals.
- Business will become less competitive and more cooperative.
- Diplomats will be less self-oriented and work more for the common good.
- The Earth will be considered in its true light as mother to humankind.
- Governments will give more power to the people.
- Court calendars will empty as judges' decisions and juries' verdicts are replaced by the application of spiritual wisdom in out-of-court settlements.
- Human relationships in love and marriage and parenting will radiate mutual understanding.
- Youngsters, when they enter the job market, will gravitate to the best job for them and for society.
- Educators will train the right-brain hemisphere and not only the left.

These are twelve daydreams about what changes will take place if we daydream more. Is this speculative? Or does our Creator deserve the credit for having a divine genius?

And is there any doubt that we all have not only the right, but the obligation, to ride on the Creator's coat-tails? A better metaphor would be the one Jesus used when referring to the meditative or daydream state: "Go to the Kingdom of Heaven within."

THE MANY PATHS TO THE HOUSE OF WISDOM

Meditation has been used by people all over the world to, as one might say, recharge their batteries.

You are using meditation when you daydream. But there is passive meditation and there is dynamic meditation. Most of the world uses passive meditation. That is, they close their eyes, relax, and go within. They do nothing else. Having shut off the material world, they are in a spiritual place. They are able to be aware of their inner self. Just by bathing in this awareness of the inner self, they are becoming closer to their spiritual source.

This type of passive meditation was the only meditation practiced until about fifty years ago. It was then that a man named José Silva discovered that a certain use of the mind while in this state of meditation produced abilities that seemed superhuman.

Any type of mind use while meditating converts passive meditation into dynamic meditation. Billions of people for thousands of years thought that this was an error. The mind should be still. But the Silva Method, requiring only four days of training, has shown that while meditation reconnects us to our spiritual source, dynamic meditation enables us to tap the abilities of that source.

Silva graduates transcend space and time in their right-brain thinking. They become psychic. They can heal. They can use dreams to solve problems. They are able to set and reach goals and manifest solutions. They are able to do everything that we can do when we visit Fairyland City.

They call it programming at the alpha level. We call it relaxing and daydreaming under control. Both actuate the right hemisphere and reconnect us to where we originally came from.

Executives of major corporations have taken the Silva training. It has been given to key personnel in management and sales by such major corporations as Mary Kay Cosmetics, RCA records, and automotive companies.

Big names among graduates include Eddie Albert; Susan Strasburg; orchestra leader Doc Severinson; Vicki Call; Shakti Gawain, author of *Creative Visualization*; Richard Bach, author of *Jonathan Livingston Seagull*; and Wayne Dwyer, author of *Red Magic*.

In her book *Living in the Light,* Shakti Gawain writes, "The most important technique I learned in that course was the basic technique of creative visualization, relaxing deeply and then picturing a desired goal in your mind exactly the way you would like to be. . . .We all do create our own reality."

Your reality is becoming a bicameral thinker due to your continued use of controlled daydreaming. The more you use it, the better you get.

One day, you will realize a stunning fact: You are clairvoyant! Perhaps you have discovered this already. Perhaps you knew something that you had no way of knowing. "Lucky guess," you probably said to yourself. No lucky guess, I assure you.

Perhaps you had a dream that turned out to be the harbinger of truth. Scary. Or somebody phoned from a distance away about whom you had just been thinking. Or you had a hunch to contact this person on the chance that . . . and you were right.

This clairvoyant or psychic faculty is a natural ability of the right brain hemisphere, which you acquire as you activate this hemisphere by controlled daydreaming. It is a natural ability of the Creator, and since you become connected to the Creator, via the right brain, it becomes a natural ability that you and the Creator share.

If you stop controlled daydreaming and become again more separated from the higher intelligence, your clairvoyant or psychic faculty will atrophy. If you don't use it, you lose it. Remember the story about the father who gave a number of talents to his sons? Those who did not use them, lost them.

Your clairvoyance is a spiritual talent. Keep it growing with frequent visits to Fairyland City, especially to the House of Wisdom, to come to major decisions. Actually, Fairyland City is not your only source of access to the House of Wisdom. Any approach to the "kingdom within" will get you there.

Certainly the Silva Method does it, and any other dynamic use of the creative right brain hemisphere. Any approach to controlled daydreaming does it also.

Other paths that lead you to the House of Wisdom may not do so in the distinct way that entering Fairyland City and spotting the spherical antenna accomplishes. But it is the same House. Not that the House of Wisdom has a number of territorial franchises. It is just not limited by its walls.

THE HOUSE OF WISDOM AND THE KINGDOM OF HEAVEN

José Silva, founder of the Silva Method, believes Jesus discovered that the source of humanity's troubles in biblical times lay in the fact that they had not learned to go within and meditate. Consequently, they were not intuitive, they were not able to prophesy, and they could not head off problems.

Silva believes that Jesus must have developed a method of mental training to correct this inability, and that this method was "The keys to enter the kingdom of heaven which Jesus gave to Peter."

Jesus says in Luke 17:21, "Neither will they say 'behold, there it is' or 'behold, here it is,' for behold, the Kingdom of God is within you."

But it seems that the keys to enter the kingdom of heaven were either hidden or lost, for nowhere in the Scriptures do we learn how to develop clairvoyance or the talent of prophecy.

Benjamin Franklin was, among many things, a lay researcher in the use of electricity. You remember his famous kite and key experiment with lightning, which later led to his invention of the lightning rod. At that time, he was accused by religionists of tampering with God's realm. He was threatened, reviled, and cursed.

Is it possible that some readers of this book will feel that we are overstepping our human limits by entering the Kingdom of God, that is, by controlled daydreaming with the purpose of becoming godly inspired?

When we are godly inspired, our guesses are right. When we are not godly inspired, our guesses could be right or wrong. God desires and inspires right. So when we guess wrong, we are not God-inspired. God, being the Creator, desires right, which indicates that wrong is not creative, but is more likely to be destructive.

By going to the House of Wisdom via the Kingdom of Heaven, we are being creative. And it is the right thing to do.

HOW ANCIENTS PERCEIVED DAYDREAMING AND NIGHTDREAMING

Dreams have always been a subject of interest and study. Ancient Greeks used to consult oracles, such as the oracle of Delphi, to ascertain the meaning of a dream.

The Toltecs, an ancient people who preceded the Aztecs in Mexico, had a number of dreaming practices both in daydreaming and in nightdreaming.

Their understanding of the dreaming process was broader than ours and included visions and shamanistic trips to the spirit world as well as daydreaming.

The Toltecs used incense burned in decorative clay pots. They would gaze into the smoke to contact the spirit world, and masks would help them to create the illusions needed to communicate with another realm.

All of this seems far out to us, but it was part of the Toltecs' daily living. They believed that every waking moment was really a dream. Their controlled daydreaming was so deep that they used it to perceive spirits around their pyramids, and to be able to communicate with them while in this deep state.

They went on to lay the groundwork for controlled nightdreaming. We are just beginning to investigate this ability. We call it lucid dreaming. It encourages the dreamer to realize, while asleep, that he or she is dreaming and can move the dream events in whatever direction wished.

There are some psychological advantages to this, but the Silva Method provides more practical techniques. Graduates of this training are able to order a dream to contain information to solve some current problems.

They have such a dream, remember it, and understand the steps it spells out for them to do.

A New Jersey minister had a successful fundraiser for a new church, with excess money that he decided to use for artwork for the entry ceilings. When the canvases arrived, he attempted to glue them to the ceiling, as other methods would damage them. But as fast as he glued them up, down they came.

He was quite embarrassed to have apparently wasted this money, but decided to use the Silva Method's dream control technique. That night, just before falling asleep, he went to his relaxed level and "ordered" a dream to solve the artwork problem.

He awoke the next morning with a clear recollection of a dream in which he was on his ladder with a hot iron and Elmer's glue. He was not particularly encouraged by this dream, as he had already unsuccessfully tried that particular glue, but nevertheless, when he got to his church, he prepared the hot iron and the glue and climbed up the ladder with a canvas.

As he glued the canvas to the ceiling, there was a sizzling sound. Apparently, the heat did something to the glue. The canvas remained on the ceiling. It is still there.

USING NIGHTDREAMS TO OBTAIN WISDOM

Wisdom can come to us through dreams.

The periodic table of elements came to its discoverer in a dream. The key characteristic of the needle that makes the automatic sewing machine possible came to its discoverer in a dream. More recently, the formula for a synthetic blood vessel that the body would not reject came to its discoverer in a dream.

Are we in communication with the spiritual realm while asleep? Is our right brain activated while asleep?

To ascertain the answer, a dream laboratory at Maimonides Hospital in Brooklyn conducted some experiments about fifty years ago. They had two measuring instruments. One measured brain waves. The other measured tiny muscle movements.

Electrodes were placed on both sides of the sleeper's head. The muscle movement detector was placed on the eyelids, as the eyelids were known to move rapidly when dreaming. This is called rapid eye movement (REM).

When the subject fell asleep, the brain waves dropped to less than four cycles per second. They remained at that frequency for nearly ninety minutes. Then the brain waves began to quicken. They leveled out again at about ten cycles per second, the same frequency that daydreaming is known to take place. At that very moment, REM was shown to start.

Dreaming took place for about fifteen minutes, and then the sleeper returned to a deep sleep—a slow brain frequency. This cycle repeated itself every ninety minutes until morning.

Nightdreaming therefore takes place at about the same brain frequency as daydreaming, when our connection to higher intelligence via the right brain hemisphere has been activated.

Yes, we can use nightdreams to obtain wisdom, and we can use the House of Wisdom to enhance our ability to do this. Here is how.

ACTION PLAN

to Get Wisdom at Night in Dreams

1. On retiring, enter Fairyland City.

2. Go to the House of Wisdom; it has a large shell antenna at the center of the roof.

3. As you enter, feel love for the divine source of wisdom.

4. Go to the center and bow your head.

5. Mentally say, "I want to have a dream tonight to help me know what to do about this problem." Mentally review the problem.

6. Express your thanks to the divine source of wisdom.

7. Leave Fairyland City.

You may awaken during the night or in the morning with a vague remembrance of a dream. Write down what you remember. As you do this, more and more details will surface. You should end up with a clear idea of what the dream is telling you.

If details are missing, or if there are parts of the dream that are hard to understand, repeat for a second night. Another dream will be remembered, perhaps with just the changes needed to make the whole meaning of the dream clear to you.

OUR OBLIGATION TO OUR CREATOR TO BE WISE

One of the first major events of our lives is one big con job—our education. You and I were given a halfway substitute for the real thing.

We were taught how to read and write. We were also taught history and some things about the world. Then came mathematics and science. All of the subjects are left brain exercises. The only right brain exercises from kindergarten through graduate university were art and music, pretty low on most curricula's budgets.

Education is a monolithic giant too inbred to ever make as large a change as from halfway to all the way.

To go all the way, educators must teach right and left brain job descriptions. Here is a brief course outline:

Left Hemisphere	Right Hemisphere
Exterior environment	Interior environment
Active	Passive
Body motion	Body language
The three Rs	Music, art
Detail	Big picture
Polarity	Unity

In analyzing these spheres of expertise, it becomes obvious that the left brain is absorbed in the material world, while the right brain is of the spiritual world, where the original oneness still exists.

Educators must also teach relaxation techniques, how to give programming to yourself or to others, the creative importance of visualization and imagination, and how to reinforce the creative power with desire, expectation, and belief, for starters.

Then should come the meat: how to use the alpha brain frequencies as produced in controlled daydreaming to solve problems, raise geniuses, reach goals, heal, and tap higher intelligence for wisdom, wisdom, wisdom.

Did you learn this in your education? Neither did I. Not only were you and I cheated, but all humanity.

I have been trying to overcome this lack in my own life and to help others do likewise. I feel we have an obligation to our Creator to live the most fairy-tale life we can.

How about you?

9

HOW TO PROTECT YOURSELF FROM CURSES AND SPELLS AND BE THE VICTOR EVERY TIME

As a person rises above the common level, perhaps because of his or her closer connection to the source of wisdom, there can be a backlash. People that are left behind often resent the success of others. They spread rumors, criticize, or blacken that name one way or another.

I have always discouraged my readers, audiences, and colleagues from making some kind of a figurehead out of me. I don't want to be crucified.

Believe it or not, people still cast spells and levy curses. These spells and curses are supported on the other side by immature entities who still get a kick out of negative wizardry.

The ancient Hawaiians had their Kahunas, good and bad. The bad were able to levy the death curse skillfully. This they brought about, it is said, by contacting a newly departed soul still trapped between this dimension and the next and promising benefits if that soul would snuff out a particular person's life force.

Doctors recognize the advent of the Kahuna's death curse. It starts with paralysis of the legs, which gradually creeps upward. Death usually comes in a week.

There are still Kahunas in Hawaii today, albeit just a few. Black magic is rare. Today's Kahunas are largely specialists in identifying healing herbs and helping the sick.

Forget Honolulu. If you live in New York, Chicago, Detroit, Miami, or even Podunk, you can still be the object of a curse or spell, sometimes emanating from a person you would least suspect. As a result, it is my duty to provide you with appropriate defense since I am responsible for providing you with the fairy-tale life that may be incurring the jealousy of others.

THE USE OF LIGHT AS AN IMPENETRABLE PSYCHIC SHIELD

The Creator is love and light. It may be asking too much of you to love the adversary who is trying to do you in. But surrounding yourself with light is quick, easy, and totally effective.

Attack can be physical or mental. Physical attack involves the use of a weapon—from fist to firearm. Light can be protection from physical attack by disarming the mind of the attacker.

When the attack is mental, with the attacker using hate thoughts, illness thoughts, curses, or spells, light acts as a barrier to their penetration of your consciousness.

Light is energy and power. Consciousness can create light. Some adepts are able to hold a fluorescent bulb in their hand and cause it to glow. All you need to do is imagine light.

Any image you hold in your mind, as in controlled daydreaming, is the shadow of things to come. Your image is the seed of creation. Your image of light creates light around you. It may not be light that throws a shadow. But it is a light that can block all shadows and evil thoughts from reaching you.

So light protects you as would an impenetrable shield. Here is what to do if you feel somebody is out to harm you.

# Action Plan

to Create a Protective Shield of Light

1. Relax.
2. Daydream, seeing yourself safe from possible enemies.
3. See the room you are in becoming lit with sunlight. The sunlight is brilliant.
4. Create an imaginary rheostat with which you can brighten the sunlight even more.
5. You are now in a room filled with brilliant white light that you can feel as a blanket of love around you.
6. When you start to feel safer than you ever felt before, turn back the rheostat.
7. End in the usual way.

CURSES AND SPELLS ORIGINATE IN THE MIND OF HUMANITY

Our Creator has given us free will. Many people who feel wronged use their free will to get even. That getting even can vary from a practical joke to the shedding of blood.

It is not God's will that this should happen. It is the will of a person.

There will be a number of Action Plans in this chapter to protect yourself from these immature actions but, because they are not spiritually caused, they do not have to be spiritually corrected. In other words, you will not have to go to Fairyland City to perform this chapter's Action Plans. They can all be done in your living room, as was the one just completed having to do with using light as protection.

Light is protection against attack. There is no power of darkness. There is only a power of light. Darkness is not a source of power, whereas light is definitely a source of power.

One jealous metaphysics practitioner we shall call Ernie knew his rival, Bert, was protecting himself against attack by surrounding himself with white light. So, this jealous metaphysician Ernie activated a weakness already existing within Bert, a sickness Bert had thought was already healed.

When a recurrence of this almost occurred, Bert realized he was being "zapped" by Ernie. He realized Ernie had bypassed the protective white light around Bert and had activated an old weakness. This required a higher energy if Bert was to successfully block Ernie's mischief.

So Bert contacted an old friend who had passed on some years ago and who had been an accomplished metaphysician. He sought his friend's higher energy. It worked. Ernie was blocked in his dastardly efforts by a stronger energy. This strength had nothing to do with Bert's late friend being on the other side, but rather was due to the power and wisdom he had attained while alive.

Your mind and consciousness can protect you from any curses, spells, and mental darts hurled at you. Because of your elevation to a higher level of consciousness and the good luck and success that comes as a result of your controlled daydreaming visits to Fairyland City, even members of your own family, not to mention neighbors, colleagues, and competitors, can begin to look at you as a threat to them.

Jealousy, envy, and resentment act as a curse. Even without the knowledge of how to levy a curse or spell, people who feel jealousy, envy, and resentment are unconsciously setting you up. These negative emotions are accompanied by negative mental pictures. Negative mental pictures tend to manifest themselves as do any of our mental pictures.

You know when this is happening. Your awareness tells you that you are resented by a particular person. You must protect yourself from that resentment, otherwise you can be prevented from producing at your maximum volume. Your creative energy can be sapped or blocked.

It takes only a minute or two to put that protection in place. It involves your daydreaming that there is a plastic envelope around you. Everything can pass through this plastic protection except negative thoughts.

Negative thoughts hit the protective covering and bounce back to where they came from. Soon the person sending you negative thoughts begins to feel tormented by them. The thoughts stop.

Here are the steps.

ACTION PLAN

to Have Curses Return to the Sender

1. Relax.
2. Daydream, seeing yourself safe from attack.
3. See yourself surrounded by a plastic-like protective shell.
4. Watch as barbs aimed at you hit the plastic and bounce back to the sender.
5. End in the usual way, knowing that only good can penetrate your protective shell.
6. At a later date, remove the plastic shell with controlled daydreaming, when you feel you are no longer under attack.

HOW PSYCHIC ATTACK CAN ORIGINATE ON THE OTHER SIDE

There are all kinds of people on earth. When people leave this plane, they go back to the creative realm from whence they came. Thousands of near-death experiences have been recorded, and most all point to the return. That means there are also all kinds of people on the other side.

A number of people on the other side, especially new arrivals, have a difficult time adjusting to the idea that they are no longer on earth. They are still attached to their earth mate or family.

This attachment or closeness tempts them to seek the earthly life energy that they had before. Without consciously knowing what they are doing, they sap your energy. They become, in effect, psychic vampires.

A person is susceptible to this kind of attack when his or her own etheric body (energy body) is being weakened by stress or illness.

Mary thought it was her female change of life that brought on this period of extreme lethargy. Once a popular socialite, she now was always in her apartment, except for brief afternoon strolls. This went on for five years. Despite medical attention, she was constantly in a state of mild depression, weariness, and disinterest.

Mary appealed to me for assistance. "I am not myself," she complained. "Is somebody doing this to me?"

Immediately I thought of psychic vampires.

"Did anyone pass away just before this started?" I asked.

She thought a moment. "Yes, a cousin who was very close to me. Why?"

I explained how those who pass on try to stay on this plane by using someone's life energy. "If this is happening, you can stop it."

"Well, let my cousin feed on me. At least I'll be doing somebody some good." It was probably this state of consciousness that made Mary a likely target for this type of psychic abuse.

With some persuasion, she agreed to take protective action. She performed the following Action Plan once a day for a week. Within two weeks, Mary became her usual active and dynamic self. She resumed traveling. Later, she confessed she even had a love affair in Greece.

ACTION PLAN

to Halt Psychic Attack
from the Other Side

1. Relax.
2. Daydream, seeing yourself safe from attack.
3. Imagine you can see the etheric body that surrounds your physical body. It is an energy field.
4. Affirm to yourself three times: "I visualize my etheric body. I strengthen its protective quality. It is now like a protective skin. No entity can invade me. I am fully protected by my strengthened etheric body."
5. End in the usual way, feeling safer and stronger.

Don't be charitable with your own life energy. Actually, the psychic vampire does not really benefit from his or her depletion of your energy. According to C. W. Leadbeater, the theosophical authority of the early part of this century, the psychic vampire is incapable of assimilating the energy he or she robs from you, so it is dissipated.

ARE YOU YOUR OWN
PSYCHIC ATTACKER?

Some people are their own worst friend. Some are even their own enemy. And some are their own psychic attackers.

You are your own worst friend when you keep telling yourself "I can't" instead of "I can," or when you put yourself down and limit your accomplishments with a perpetually poor self-image. You are Mr. "What If?" Color yourself gray.

You are your own enemy when you keep visualizing the worst instead of the best. You are putting creative energy into problems and bringing them into fruition instead of solutions. You are "Mr. Yes, But." Color yourself brown.

You are your own psychic attacker when you fear psychic attack. You are your own psychic attacker when you dwell on morbid possibilities, think of suicide, crime, and murder, or take drugs to escape. You then are "Mr. No Way Out." Color yourself black.

You can tell who among your friends are their own psychic attackers. They bring the conversation around to financial crises, atomic wars, or earthquakes. If *The Exorcist* is playing in the next town, they'll drive the twenty miles to see it, even though they have seen it three times already. They are the Chicken Littles, ever warning that the sky is falling.

Psychic self-attackers who go the drug route damage themselves the most. If they have not gone beyond the point of no return, they create a leak in their etheric body that takes a long time to heal.

You can tell if somebody is losing life energy as a result of a present or past drug habit. Put your left hand over their head—no need to touch them. You will feel a warmth or a tingle on your left palm as you search for a possible leak. To search, move your hand in a sweeping motion from ear to ear, just above the hair and then from the crown to the nape of the neck. Be aware of any heat or tingling in your palm.

Helping such a person is possible if it is only a slight tingle or warmth leakage. Strong tingling or heat feelings at a cranial point could indicate that a person has already self-inflicted irreparable harm.

There is little point in making psychic corrections if the etheric body is to be damaged again and again by further drug usage; however, if such usage is discontinued, you can help repair that person's etheric body by having that person perform the previous Action Plan to halt psychic attack from the other side.

If you are your own psychic attacker, again, light is your best answer. However, besides surrounding yourself in mental light, you also need to surround yourself in physical light.

Some of the directly physical ways have already been listed for you on page 72. You should also consider these indirect physical ways to bring even more light into your life:

- Associate with positive, enthusiastic people, avoiding negative pessimists.
- Emphasize fresh fruits and vegetables in your diet, switching from dense food such as beef and pork.
- Get plenty of sleep, making sure that thoughts of serenity and assurance prevail at the time of relaxation prior to sleep.
- Perform Action Plans daily that surround you in brilliant white light, as described earlier, or entail a visit to Fairyland City.
- Help other people to become more positive. Do so in a gentle, loving way.

PROPER BEHAVIOR FOR A PERSON READY TO LIVE A FAIRY-TALE LIFE

You have developed the skill of relaxing body and mind and daydreaming with a purpose in this relaxed way. With this skill, you have learned to become closer to the source of your creation and to thereby heighten your consciousness. Your heightened consciousness has placed you where you have earned assistance from your Creator's messengers, handmaidens, servants, and magicians—their presence invited by your visits to Fairyland City.

You are an enlightened person. You now lead a charmed life. Old habits of behavior characteristic of your old self have slipped away. Otherwise, they would tend to hold you in your old lower state of consciousness. With these old habits gone, new ones must take their place.

This will happen naturally for most enlightened readers. But others will need help. I can give this help not by listing no-longer-needed behavior patterns, but rather by pointing in the direction of behavior factors that tend to reinforce the consciousness that is rising and befit the enlightened ones.

By definition, these rules for enlightened living are also rules for psychic protection. As they go about elevating your consciousness, they lift you out of reach of lower forces.

Seven Suggestions to Elevate Consciousness

1. Attune yourself to higher energies. If you permit your mind to dwell on possession, black magic, evil witches, and other negatives, you are on their wavelength.

2. Direct your spiritual queries to a specific source. When you ask to see the future, for instance, ask your Higher Self, or God, or some specific high entity. To broadcast queries widely invites pranksters to reply.

3. Mind your own business. Do not attempt to enter somebody else's dispute, health problem, or other situation without being invited. Trespass invites trespass in return.

4. Remain in possession of your senses. Dulling the senses with alcohol, drugs, or other materials creates the vacuum that psychic invaders watch for.

5. Guard your health. Proper nutrition, proper exercise, and proper sleep keeps up your resistance to psychic attack as well as physical invaders.

6. Daydream regularly. Daily picturing of white light and attunement to the Highest creates protection.

7. Think "protection." Feel safe and you are safe. Fear attack and you open yourself to it!

HOW TO WIN DOWN-TO-EARTH ARGUMENTS IN A SPIRITUAL WAY

How do you love an adversary? How do you understand someone whose ideas are diametrically opposed to yours? How can you feel a closeness with somebody who might even be your enemy? And how in the world can you be equitable and just when your need is pressing?

These are apparently contradictions. But not to the spiritually connected.

You have seen yourself operate on a plane of apparent contradictions doing the work in previous chapters—contradicting the laws of physics regarding space and time and communications. You have actually risen above these laws by going into a mental level—a level where different laws operate, laws that might be quite opposite to physical laws.

Let me give you an example. You have experienced the pull of magnets. A magnet has two ends, or poles. If you place the north pole of one magnet near the south pole of another magnet, the two are attracted to each other and pulled together. On the other hand, if you put the north end of each magnet together, they repel each other. On the physical level, opposites attract. Likes repel.

What about laws on the mental level? Are you attracted to people who are different than you? People who look different, dress different, talk different, think different? Of course not. You prefer to be with people you can relate to, and you are more likely to prefer a member of the opposite sex (physical level) with whom you have common interests and beliefs (mental level).

So, you temporarily shelve this physical plane in order to activate the five rules for winning an argument—that is, convincing somebody miles away to see things your way on a more spiritual level. Then you go to work on the mental plane.

We have covered ways of protecting yourself from both physical and mental attack. But as an enlightened soul, you need to be aware of the new tools available to you to combat everyday confrontations and arguments.

These tools are mental, with a sound spiritual basis. Let's concentrate on these most important five: love, understanding, reason, need, and rapport. Here is how to use these five to help you win arguments.

Love. Despite our physical differences, we are people. Despite our separateness, we are all parts of humanity: one person pollutes, all people suffer; one person is charitable, all people are elevated. See this common ground between the two of you. Ignore the differences; dwell on the similarities. If you take a moment to do this right now, you will get a warm feeling within a few seconds.

Understanding. You are the way you are because of your upbringing, learning, and environmental input. He is the way he is because of his upbringing, his learning, and his environmental input— all different from yours. If you have a right to be the way you are, does not he have the right to be the way he is? Take a moment now to feel his right to be as he is, to understand him.

Reason. Reason is a two-way street. First, see the reasonability of the other person's stand. It is not yours, it is his. Now mentally review the reasonability of your stand. There are pros and cons in each stand. Review how the pros minus the cons for your stand compare to the pros minus the cons for his stand. Become reason-oriented to the problem.

Need. Think of your need in terms of how many problems could be solved if your need was met. How about secondary problems? When one problem is solved, usually others fade away, too. Involve as many people as you can in the chain of happiness that will result when your need is filled.

Rapport. Now permit all the positive feelings about this person to enter and to eclipse the feelings of hostility and antagonism. You are working together on this problem—on a higher level.

When you apply these five rules to your handling of everyday conflicts, the conflicts have a way of resolving themselves. It often seems like magic, or like a higher intelligence has intervened.

It has.

When the parties or party to a conflict is a distance away, you can use your controlled daydreams to transcend this distance. Here is how to win an argument at a distance.

ACTION PLAN

to Win an Argument at a Distance

1. Have a photo of the person on your lap.
   If no photo is available, make a pencil sketch
   of the person.

2. Relax.

3. Daydream, seeing yourself with the person.

4. Activate the five rules given above, one at a time.
   As you present your side, open your eyes to look
   at the photo or sketch as you start to apply each
   of the five rules. You need look for only a few
   seconds before closing your eyes again.

5. Ask the person to agree to your stand as it has
   been presented with love, understanding, reason,
   need, and rapport.

6. Open your eyes to look at the photo or sketch
   and mentally see the person agreeing with you.

7. Review your true feelings—love, understanding,
   reason, need, and rapport.

8. End your daydreaming session in the usual way,
   knowing that the differences have been resolved.

HOW SCIENCE LOOKS AT THE SHIFT IN CONSCIOUSNESS YOU ARE MAKING

This chapter has been a detour from Fairyland City because your trips there in previous chapters have done something to you.

What has happened is you have become a more aware being. To your friends and family, you appear more interested in them. A mate notices it first. Perhaps you have said the words "I love you" for the first time in what has seemed like an eon. The children notice it, too. Perhaps you have played catch with them for the first time or taken them to the zoo. Your colleagues at work have noticed the change in you, too. Perhaps you are willing to help them more, to pitch in on projects that are not your responsibility, or to stay overtime if you are needed.

As these initial signs of your progress are succeeded by additional advances in the growth of your level of consciousness, then the measures offered you in this chapter to protect yourself become more essential to you.

What has actually happened? If you ask me this question, I am tempted to answer in what seems to be biblical terms. This is because what has happened is not physical in nature, but rather it is spiritual in nature.

Abide with me now as I explain in the language of religion what has happened to you. I will then make an attempt to use science's language to answer the same question. First, religion's terminology.

All your life you have been wishing for a cure-all to all of life's problems. You have been hoping that an easy-to-swallow remedy would suddenly appear to give you wisdom, health, financial security, confidence, and harmony in your relationships. Perhaps this remedy would appear in the form of the good fairy, or your guardian angel, or even . . . .

Well, it has! Thanks to the good fairy, and your guardian angel, you are closer to God. God's love for you and your love for God has been magnified. It has made you whole.

With this divine love surging through your veins and filling every cell in your consciousness, you can do all things. You receive divine ideas, rich ideas that increase your awareness of prosperity and the universal abundance around you.

This divine love attracts loving people into your life, people with the same spiritual light that shines from you. Your whole life begins to reflect your love of God and God's love of you. And now . . . .

I promised to give you science's understanding of the changes that you have brought about in yourself by controlled daydreaming and visits to Fairyland City. Here it is.

Science has been taken out of the laboratory in recent years where it has been hiding from the concept of consciousness and had its collective face rubbed in it.

Scientists have stood by while people have walked on hot coals and not been burned. They have watched as some have stood in the fire for half an hour or have had shovels of burning hot coals spilled over their head in a fiery shower with no injury.

They have seen firsthand how, in primitive societies, stray cattle have been located by controlled daydreaming, using a psychic skill known as remote viewing. They have persons who have developed a skill known as psychometry accurately describe the owner of an object that they are given to hold in their hand. They have watched as persons moved objects across a table with the power of their mind.

Scientists watched yogis in India control bodily processes consciously when these processes were accepted by the scientists as uncontrollable. Within a few years, with the help of biofeedback training, western people were learning how to do this too.

So it has been with scientists that old belief systems have been discarded and a new view of the world has been gradually replacing them.

Perhaps Roger Sperry put it into words best. He was the winner of a 1981 Nobel Prize for his human brain studies. In a paper titled "Changing Priorities," he wrote: "Current concepts of the mind-brain relation involve a direct break with the long-established materialist and behaviorist doctrine. . . . Instead of renouncing or ignoring consciousness, the new interpretation gives full recognition to the primacy of inner conscious awareness as a causal reality."

Why not substitute for "inner conscious awareness" the words "controlled daydreaming"?

Yes, controlled daydreaming is slowly being recognized as a causal reality.

So everything in the religious terminology is really not in conflict with the scientific viewpoint. It just uses different words.

When the love of God is in your consciousness, you are truly creating a loving life for yourself.

There is no conflict between science and religion. You can lead a fairy-tale life.

CAN THE INTERNET TAKE YOU TO A HIGHER CONSCIOUSNESS?

It would seem as you got closer to a million human units of consciousness that you would grow in consciousness.

The largest system serving e-mail messengers is the Internet. It is a worldwide linking of millions of computers. How many millions? Perhaps ten to twenty.

These millions of people can put a notice on an electronic bulletin board that they can all read. Each person can write another person whose computer address they have. Each person can join in a "real time" session, which is an actual conversation, typing one line at a time.

One morning on Senior Net, a woman who was a regular came on garbled. Finally, she typed "I'm IN TROUBLE." When a sender uses capital letters this way, it is like screaming. She signed "Ilene." One person who knew her address called 911 and then called Ilene and kept her talking. She was suffering from an overdose of medicine. The police arrived and took care of the problem. Ilene's story was told on National Public Radio, and Ilene was quoted later in *Reader's Digest* as saying, "I've found a community of people who know and love me—plus my world is expanded. . . . I'm like an elderly surfer on the first big wave of cyberspace and it's a great feeling."

Signing on and saying hello are part of a daily routine. It's like meeting your neighbors in the backyard. Some discuss their wives, their boyfriends, their kids. No small amount of flirting is done and cyberspace is filled with sexual innuendoes. Many consider cyberspace part of a revolution taking place that's bound to affect all Americans profoundly.

I am not one of those many. I agree it is a *revolution* in communication, but I doubt if it has anything to do with *evolution.*

Yes, you get closer to a lot of people. But chances are, the average level of consciousness is no different than yours. So you are not lifted by that closeness.

What is the level of consciousness of fairies, angels, and the rest of God's messengers? Yes, the answer is much higher. And because it is higher, any contact with them, in or out of Fairyland City, is a blessing to your consciousness.

We don't blame anyone for being wide-eyed and entranced by being able to participate in the workings of the minds of so many other people. In the process of doing that, you expand you own life's experiences.

Don't you have all you can do to handle your own life? You cannot give somebody you know in cyberspace a fairy-tale life. But you can acquire such a life yourself.

It is not by typing messages into your computer.

It is by daydreaming controlled mental trips into the land of God's messengers.

10

HOW TO STAY ON THE GOOD SIDE OF THE OTHER SIDE

"This book has as its origin the conviction that an essential part of man's duty upon earth is to bear witness to the truth as it has been revealed to him." So does John G. Bennett begin his book called *Witness* (Dharma Book Company, Inc., 1962), in which he discusses the forces that shaped his early life, including the effects on him of the teachings of Gurdjeff and Ouspensky, both contemporary, innovative philosophers.

Since I endorse this concept and claim it as the motivating force behind my book, too, I start this final chapter with that idea.

I would like to go a step further and recount one of Bennett's experiences, as it, too, dovetails with the ideas and teachings herein.

In 1947, Bennett returned to Coombe Springs, a town outside of London, England, where he had lived as a boy. For the first time in thirty years, he visited his old Kings College School. As he walked through the grounds, past the laboratories, and over the playing field where for two years he had captained the rugby team, he came upon a memorial to those lost in World War I.

Stopping to read the names, he came upon one name after another of boys with whom he had played rugby or cricket. No wonder he had not returned before. How could he ever reconcile himself to the loss of so many of his best friends? Hardly a one seemed to have escaped.

"I was all alone in the great playing field, but as I stood, I was no longer alone. All these boys were still there; still living, with their powers undiminished. A Great Presence enveloped us all. An immense joy flooded through me."

Bennett described that Presence. "That day, Coombe Springs was visited by some Great Presence. It might have been some angel or an even greater Being. . . . I was, during the whole of that day, completely certain that in some utterly incomprehensible way, the boys who had been with me at school and had died on the battlefield were as much alive as I was. . . . I discovered, as the days went by, that several others had been aware of a Great Presence and of a blessing that had come to us."

The main lesson to Bennett of this experience was, in his words, "Potentialities are not destroyed by death."

The main lesson to me is, "We are not alone."

In his preface, Bennett apologizes for having presumed to write as though he had been privilege to a vision not shown to others. "It happens that I am almost wholly deficient in visual imagery, and I have been astonished in recent years to find this power awakened in me."

In this last chapter, as largely in the entire book, we are going to presume we are not alone. We are going to presume also that by now the power of visual imagery has been awakened in us. And based on the truth of these assumptions, we are going to use our visual imagery to stay in close companionship with our celestial companions.

HOW DO YOU SEE YOURSELF TODAY?

What is your vision of yourself? What are your thoughts right now about your beliefs, your capabilities, and your health? How do you see yourself today?

The answers to this question today determine how you will be tomorrow.

The reason is that these answers comprise the climate in which your brain and body cells are reproducing. Healthy climate—healthy brain cells, healthy body cells. Poor climate—unhealthy brain cells, unhealthy body cells.

Your thoughts and beliefs about yourself are creating the pattern for your continuing self. They do so by governing the climate in which these cells are renewing themselves.

To lead a fairy-tale life, you need to maintain a fairy-tale life vision for yourself. You must raise your current thoughts and beliefs about yourself, your life, and your health. Certainly, you must raise your vision from disease to wholeness.

We can always take a lesson from Jesus. When Jesus said to the man in the temple, "Stretch out your hand" (Mt. 12:13), he did not see a withered hand. He saw a hand filled with life, with strong muscles, nerves, and tendons. He maintained a vision of wholeness for that hand, and those visions became true.

We are about to perform an Action Plan that will give you a chance to see yourself perfect. But before you do this Action Plan, I insist that you practice holding this perfect picture in your controlled daydreaming.

In fact, when you think you have a pretty near perfect picture of yourself, improve it. When you have improved it, improve it again.

Why am I so insistent on a picture that depicts you at your ultimate best? Because as you see yourself in the Action Plan, so you will become.

I want this Action Plan to lift you by your bootstraps and send you soaring! If I have my way, you will become a spiritual giant. You will find yourself looked up to as a leader. You will naturally display a genius intellect, a superhuman wisdom, and a dazzling personality.

How about a little friendly coaching before you begin? Suppose we take a look at the picture you have of the ultimate you and see if it could use a little touching up. Relax and daydream now. Create the perfect picture of yourself. Then we'll talk some more. Go ahead. I'll wait. . . .

Let me give you a checklist and you can use it to make sure the picture you just made includes all of these qualities.

- You are healthy.
- Your posture is erect.
- Your thoughts are positive.
- You have overwhelming love.
- You are aware of your spiritual nature.
- You are aware of your sexual nature.
- Your habits are all good.
- Your weight is normal.
- Your attitude is optimistic.
- You are patient and tolerant.
- You are radiant.
- You are surrounded by admirers.

Remember, these are not qualities that you need to have now. You would probably miss by a mile, no insult intended. It is just that rare is the person who can attain all of these qualities or develop them in a lifetime.

You will attain them. See. Believe. Know. You will have help in attaining this position of stardom in humanity. Help will come from You-Know-Who.

HOW TO MAKE YOUR IDEAL SELF-IMAGE MANIFEST NOW

What you are about to do has the unanimous support of all the powers that be. You have decided to live a life that is the closest to perfection that you can conceive. Can anybody object to that on this side or the other side?

As a result of this unanimity, you can perform the next Action Plan anywhere in Fairyland City that you prefer. When you enter via the garden and get your key, you can stop right there and hold your ideal self-image in your controlled daydream in the garden.

Or you can visualize the Eternal Life Health Spa, or the Universal Bank. Your choice includes the Universal Trade Center, The Supreme Court, or the House of Wisdom.

Wherever you decide to spend a minute holding in mind your ideal self-image, you have the support of the divine messengers there. The only consideration that might make one Fairyland City facility more advisable than another is the specific self-image aspect you need to work on.

In what department did your picture need touching up? If it had to do with health, you should choose as your locale for this Action Plan the Eternal Life Health Spa. If it had to do with difficulty in picturing yourself wealthy, choose the Universal Bank. Or maybe you could not see yourself as a genius, so you would do this Action Plan in the House of Wisdom.

Wherever you choose, this trip to Fairyland City will change your life!

ACTION PLAN

to Manifest Your Ideal Self-Image

1. Relax.

2. Daydream.

3. With the doorway to Fairyland City enveloped in your bright white light, walk in.

4. Go to the garden and get your key from the drop of water in one of the roses that reflects all the colors.

5. Stay in the garden or go to any Fairyland City facility where you feel it is best for you to be.

6. Count backwards from 10 to 1 to deepen your relaxation.

7. See yourself as magnificently as you can imagine yourself to be, using the perfected image you have practiced holding before.

8. Permit this image to fade when it wants to, but bring it back time after time until you feel you have held this image a total of one minute.

9. Lower your head in thanks, love, and respect for the angels, fairies, and other powers that be.

10. Leave Fairyland City via the garden, where you return your key.

11. Pass through the doorway, leaving it open and mentally affirming, "My consciousness is one with universal consciousness. Universal life energy surges through me as I go forth."

12. Open your eyes, feeling great. Every morning on arising, relax and see yourself as your ideal self-image.

Congratulations! I bow my head to you in thanks, love, and respect for your having lifted yourself up, in effect by your bootstraps, in order to be able to heighten your contribution to world society and to the meaningfulness of your life.

NEW ABILITIES THAT YOU CAN NOW EXPECT

We are all unique beings.

Some of us are more sensitive with the sense of sight, others with the sense of hearing. When those who are more sensitive to the sense of sight begin to manifest their more perfect self, they can become seers. They can "see" with their mind's eye what is happening thousands of miles away. They are optically psychic. When the sound-sensitive mature, they can hear voices relating answers to questions. They are audio-psychic.

So you may now become clairvoyant or you may become clairaudient, depending on your natural abilities. Both are great advantages. One thing is sure—you are becoming more psychic. Your controlled daydreaming will be able to serve you in ways that you have not thought possible.

Your metaphysical powers are increasing. You are becoming more and more able to cause life energy to flow through your body for astounding endurance.

Your wisdom is already immeasurable. You have the judgment to make the right decision time after time.

Some grow faster than others and in one department rather than another.

Expect all of this for yourself. Keep that picture of your ideal self active in your mind. Feel exhilarated about yourself. Here are some of the improvements that can occur and some of the abilities that can be acquired.

- You will know how to handle a troublesome teenager, an unfaithful mate, a malicious gossiper, an unethical competitor, an unpleasant co-worker, a pesky neighbor.

- You will express naturally more understanding, empathy, oneness, rapport, love, peace, and harmony.

- You will use your mind to communicate with your body to improve your health and maintain a high level of wellness.

- You will accelerate your success, function with a high degree of accuracy in intuitive matters, and be a source of creative and innovative ideas.

- You will become more influential, magnify your attraction to the opposite sex, and be looked up to as a mentor by many.

How much is the above worth to you? Well, there is a price you must pay: You must see that picture of your ideal self at least once a day in your controlled daydreams.

If you look back over your progress in this book, first you cleared out negative blocks that were standing in your way, money being one of them. Next, in effect, you created room in your life for good things to happen. Now you are ready for the big prizes spelled out above.

But you must keep that picture of the special you on the front burner until you are convinced you have fully arrived.

A public relations man in his early forties was just scraping by. It was tough going to get newspapers to accept stories about his restaurant clients and other commercial ventures that he was paid to get publicity for. He found he had to pull off stunts like getting a local circus to paint one of the elephants white and walk it on Main Street for a Chamber of Commerce "White Elephant Sale Day."

"There must be a better way to make a living than this," he thought to himself. I taught him the art of cosmic attunement and re-creation by picturing a new self. He practiced this daily for a few weeks.

Then things started to happen. He was called in by the local school system. They needed the education story told to the local community to create support for the program when budget voting time came around. He was retained on an annual basis. Another board of education heard about him, then another. The mayor of his town retained him to help with the town image. Within a year, he had a half dozen of these high-paying governmental clients, valid sources of new and higher levels of uses for his public relations talents.

No more stunts and circuses, and a lot more money.

The change spread to his married life. A new son, a new contemporary home, a new career. Then came offers of political office and . . . I wish I know how far he went, but I left that area and lost track of his glorious transformation.

Such is the transformation that can be yours.

HOW TO TRIGGER YOUR MIND TO WORK FOR YOU AUTOMATICALLY

Mental pictures are creative. Have I said that enough? No. It needs to be embossed on our brains. But here is something I have not told you: Physical pictures can trigger mental pictures and themselves become creative.

A professional mentalist, who worked in European nightclubs before World War II, was able to read the serial numbers on money while still in the purses and wallets of patrons. He performed two shows a night, illustrating this remarkable psychic ability.

One night after his second show, two soldiers in German military uniform approached him.

"Do you do private shows?" one asked him.

"Yes," he replied. "If the price is right."

"You will do this one free," they affirmed with authority. "You will perform for Adolph Hitler in his office at Bergdesgarten."

It was an overnight automobile ride. When they arrived, the mentalist was escorted through long hallways in order to reach Hitler's office. He noticed large photographs lining one wall. These photographs were of famous buildings in various capitals of Europe. On each building was a swastika.

Every time Hitler entered or left his office, whether he looked at the photos or not, he was being programmed like a computer to take over these capitals.

Eventually, he did.

How would you like to do the same? No, not win capitals of Europe and then lose your life. But how would you like to create your own collection of pictures that will program you to reach your goals?

Metaphysicians have used such pictures for centuries. They are often called "treasure maps."

I have one in front of me. There is a picture of a luxury ocean liner. A new compact car. A luscious piece of chocolate cake. A newspaper with a photo and article. And a large audience listening to a lecture.

This was a person's treasure map. He placed it on his bathroom door where he knew he would see it several times a day.

Within a year, he had his cruise, his new compact car, and had enjoyed the most delicious chocolate cake imaginable. He gave two seminars that were totally sold out, but rather than have anyone turned away, he had extra seats placed on the stage with him. After one of these, he was interviewed by a reporter and the Sunday magazine section had a two-page spread about him with a photo in color.

I can vouch for the accuracy of this example of the magic of treasure maps, as the map I described was mine and the treasure it developed was mine too.

Simple Steps to Make Your Treasure Map

1. Start to clip pictures from color magazines that illustrate your heart's desire. When you have four to eight, get a piece of cardboard or sheet of paper large enough to hold them as backing.

2. Glue the pictures to the backing.

3. Mount the backing on your refrigerator or other well-frequented spot in your house.

4. Stare at the treasure map. Repeat the universal sound "OM" three times.

5. From now on, whenever daydreaming, recall the details of your treasure map and see it where you hung it in your house.

Warning: Do not put anything on your treasure map that you have any doubt about having. The certainty factor about it arriving is quite high.

AS YOU BECOME MORE IMPORTANT, YOU MUST BETTER YOUR INTER-PERSONAL COMMUNICATION SKILLS

You may be leading a fairly private life now but, as your ideal self-image manifests, you will probably find things changing.

What needs to be prepared for contacts with all kinds of other people are your abilities to get your ideas across with understanding and rapport.

Spiritually, your mind is being prepared for this by the other side, but interpersonal communication skills are a material world activity and need your attention at a material world level of awareness.

This does not mean that controlled daydreaming and Fairyland City will not help you. To the contrary, they will be of immeasurable help. In fact, they will make it possible for you to accomplish your communication skills acquisition practically overnight.

For decades, the Russians have had a way to help artists and writers increase their talents by leaps and bounds. It was a simple process. A composer would pick a famous composer, past or present, and daydream about what he or she looked like and imagine hearing one of their typical works. Their own work then took on an unmistakable similarity.

José Silva, founder of the Silva Method, was invited to lecture to an association of artists in Amarillo, Texas, back in 1967, just as he was launching his mind training course.

One artist, a neophyte, asked, "How can I improve my painting?"

"Are you willing to relax and follow my instructions?"

After an enthusiastic yes, José asked this young lady, "What painter would you like to emulate in your painting?"

"Van Gogh," she replied.

José then had her close her eyes and relax. He gave her instructions on how to deepen her relaxation. When she was deeply relaxed, he instructed her to imagine she was painting a copy of a Van Gogh painting. The class watched as she moved her hands through the air as if she was painting.

When she stopped, José told her, "All you need to do to have Van Gogh advise you on a future work is to put your three fingers together and see the image of Van Gogh."

José asked her to open her eyes and paint something. She got up and painted a vase with flowers in it. The class was aghast at its resemblance to a Van Gogh work. Just then, an art instructor entered the room to monitor the lecture. He walked up to the painting and began to point out similarities to a Van Gogh!

Communication is an art. Master this art and you gain in stature and power. You become a better co-creator. Here are some of the advantages that you can gain.

- Cut down on friction at home and at work.
- Get people's respect, attention, and support.
- Radiate warmth and caring, making people feel safe about opening up to you.
- Become automatically polished in body language—its position and movement.
- Become automatically skilled in tone and inflection.
- Express yourself clearly the first time around— no explaining or repeating.
- Be comfortable about thinking and speaking on your feet.
- Connect with all kinds of people, getting across to types with whom you may have had problems before.
- Become more influential as your ideas are accepted more readily.

All of this you will accomplish by attending a few lectures or talks by skilled speakers and listening while in a daydreaming state. Here are the steps to follow.

ACTION PLAN

to Better Your Communication Skills

1. Attend talks, lectures, or workshops by a person or persons whose presentation skills you admire.
2. At each event, study the facial features as the lecturer talks; close your eyes and practice.
3. With eyes closed, listen to the lecturer's voice: how emphasis is attained, use of tone and inflection, et cetera. Do this for a total of a few minutes.
4. In between events, take one imaginary trip to Fairyland City as per previous instructions, getting your key and remaining there.
5. In Fairyland City's garden, see yourself speaking to an audience and projecting all of the characteristics of the speaker(s) whose talks you attended.

YOU CAN IMPROVE OTHER SKILLS IN THE SAME WAY

Can you see yourself impressing people right off the bat? Can you see yourself fitting in with any group from the very start? Can you see yourself exercising leadership in your family, community, and job?

These questions should evoke a quick and easy yes. If not, practice these pictures until you become more and more comfortable with them and they become more and more natural to you.

These mental pictures of your responding to your communication skills have another advantage.

You do not want to be a clone of somebody else. You want to be uniquely yourself. So when you continue to use mental pictures of yourself with the same expertise as the speaker(s) you chose to emulate, you can now add a quality that is strictly yourself.

This is an important step. The Creator, with whom you are now closer than ever before, created you as a unique person. So do you want to continue to be unique?

You can use the emulation of a speaker to advance your communication skills as a model for advancing other skills that you now feel are needed as you grow into your ideal self-image.

Perhaps one of the skills you need to advance is your skill at attracting the opposite sex. A sexually frustrated person is blocking his or her own spiritual growth. Those who are happily married or satisfactorily expressing their sexual nature can skip the next sub-heading.

The rest of you, read on.

HOW TO TURN UP YOUR SEXUAL ATTRACTION

Just as interpersonal communications is a neutral skill that helps you manifest your ideal self-image, so is the expression of your sexual nature. So many social taboos interfere with learning how to get out from under our inhibitions in this area that many of us take these inhibitions to our grave.

You can turn up your sexual attraction by observing the characteristics of sexually attractive people and then using controlled daydreaming and seeing yourself that way. Here again, you combine the physical with the spiritual.

What are such characteristics?

Perhaps a seated woman leans casually on her elbow, swinging her crossed leg; or perhaps a woman leans closely to a man she just met, her shoulder touching his.

Perhaps a man stands nonchalantly, his thumbs hooked under his belt, fingers pointing down; or perhaps he stands looking off into space, ignoring everybody around him.

What are these two really saying with their body language? They are both saying that they have something. That something is super sexual self-confidence.

Even if they don't really have it, they can still express it by subtle body language. Even if they do not have super sexual self-confidence, by permitting it to be subtly expressed, they can enhance their power of attraction manyfold.

Confidence speaks sexual reams. The confident male inspires confidence in the female and vice versa. A few minutes of controlled daydreaming, acting out the part of a sexually confident person, will get you to radiate a man or woman of the world charisma. This is true even if you know deep inside you're as green as an unripe apple.

A simple thing like the aperture of your eyes can make a change in your acceptance by others. This is taught in many executive training courses. You may as well acquire this impressive trait.

ACTION PLAN

to Gain Acceptance with Your Eyes

1. When you wish to hold the attention of a listener, or to influence a member of the opposite sex, hold eye contact a bit longer than usual.

2. Open the aperture of the eyes slightly. Do not stare, but move your eyes closer to staring.

3. After a few minutes of conversation in which you apply steps 1 and 2, express your wish or the purpose of the conversation. Very likely, it will be agreed to.

When you do this Action Plan, adding sexual attraction to your ideal self-image, repeating it once a day for a few days, you become your ideal self-image.

Any improvement you make in yourself via your controlled daydreaming is not only a physical improvement, but it is a spiritual improvement.

The Creator makes us perfect. Then we mature and go out in the physical world and the you-know-what hits the fan. As you acquire all sorts of negative fears and self-limitations, you express a fearsome, limited being—hardly as the Creator meant you to be.

When somebody sees you and their eyes light up, you know they are glad to see you. On the other hand, when a person is angry, the eyes narrow to slits. People will respond to the ways that you use your eyes.

Maybe what have been social and sexual fiascoes for you in the past can now be crescendo after crescendo of ecstatic success.

TAKING CHARGE OF YOUR OWN WELLNESS

The ideal self-image is one of health. No matter how else you see yourself growing in self-mastery, you need to have a picture of yourself when you daydream in which you radiate youth, energy, and vitality.

You have angels assisting you in reaching your highest self-image. They are on the other side, but in your great effort to become the ultimate you, they are on your side.

However, they can't eat for you, or sleep for you, or limber up for you. Here are twelve of the areas in which it is totally your responsibility to maintain a high level of wellness.

- Pray and meditate daily.

- Exercise a half hour every day.

- Favor more whole grains, fruits, and vegetables, and less fatty meats.

- Drink a quart or more of pure water a day, in addition to other fluids.

- Keep all three elimination systems in active working order—kidneys, bowels, sweat glands.

- Favor cotton and other natural fibers in your clothing.

- Move away from lengthy, stressful situations.

- Love, love, love.

- See the humor in even the grimmest situations and have jokes galore ready to tell.

- Be philosophical about difficulties. Say, "This too shall pass." And believe it.

- Get plenty of sleep. "Plenty" differs for people, but varies between six and ten hours.
- Helping others is good for you. Help somebody every day.

HOW TO STAY ON THE GOOD SIDE OF THE OTHER SIDE

I may have pulled a fast one on you.

Everything in this chapter has been aimed at having you attain your fullest potential, but attaining your fullest potential is the supreme hope for you of the guardian angels, good fairies, and God's other helpers.

So as you daydream to begin to manifest your ideal self-image, they are in the wings rooting for you and applauding your every success.

You are doing exactly what you need to do to remain on the good side of the other side.

Many self-help teachers, including those who emphasize spiritual growth, give you earthshaking ways to make this a better world to live in.

They see you emptying the battlefields of war, the prisons of criminals, and the hospitals of the sick. These are all good goals for you to have, goals that automatically put the other side on your side, keeping you in the eye of the angels.

But if you do an Action Plan that makes you a better communicator, what angels, fairies, and celestial magicians are not totally with you? Anything you do to help manifest in your life the ultimate you is God's work. And to keep the other side supporting you, all you need to do is God's work. And God and God's heavenly co-workers are your helpers. Self-improvement is a path to leading a fairy-tale life.

Once you have made strides in self-improvement, especially with the use of controlled daydreaming, you will receive God's words in a clearer, more understandable way. You will receive intuitive guidance to new ideas, unique solutions to problems, and even money-making inventions.

But you have to be listening.

HOW ONE PERSON LISTENED TO GOD'S SECRETS AND PATENTED THEM

The universe speaks to you through people, events, signs, dreams, and omens. Some people even hear voices. Others are not listening at all.

When we do not listen to another person talking, it is probably because we are totally concerned with our own problems of the moment. Or instead of trying to understand what is being said, we are already preparing our reply, or we are judging or reacting to preconceptions and prejudices.

We need to practice listening to other people, and then we will become more skilled at listening to our own intuition—the spiritual guidance that we have generated through controlled daydreaming and visits to Fairyland City.

At midnight on July 9, 1856, a boy was born to a Serbian Orthodox minister and his wife in Croatia, now part of Yugoslavia. To Nikola Tesla, even childhood seemed to be in frequent meditation. When only five, he invented a water wheel and a new kind of fish hook.

When Nikola was seven, firemen in the town were trying to pump water from the river for use on a fire, but no water came. Nikola, who was even then listening to the intelligence of the universe, suddenly dived into the river and removed an obstruction that had crimped the hose.

Soon Tesla, in his twenties, invented and patented the first AC motor, which he sold to George Westinghouse for a million dollars plus a partnership. Tesla went on to invent the wireless broadcast of radio waves, the turbine engine, and fluorescent lighting. He listened, invented, and patented.

But then the universe began to tell him secrets that humankind did not accept, such as a way to charge up the earth so anyone could plug into it and get power. He was rejected by other scientists. He withdrew from society. So sensitive was he that he could feel the rejections as negative energy. He could feel other people's pain and emotions. He lived his last years as a recluse, insulating his hypersensitive attunement from both society and the universe.

Was the universe at fault in sharing secrets with Tesla that were not accepted? Or had Tesla been lax in improving his own ability at interpersonal communications?

See how one person's lapse in the process of self-improvement can set back world progress? Had Tesla read this chapter and done the simple things set forth to hold attention and communicate convincingly, we might all be enjoying an infinite source of power sans pollution or monthly electric bills.

HOW TO IMPROVE YOUR
INTUITIVE HEARING

There is a simple finger position that, when properly programmed into your mental computer through controlled daydreaming, will act as a trigger device to improve your listening to the inner intelligence we call intuition.

Used in a number of Eastern cultures, it consists of placing the thumb and forefinger together to form a circle. It is said to close your energy circuit so you are unable to transmit but free to receive. Symbolically, it unites your will with Universal will, thus tuning you to this highest of all "stations" and inviting intuitive reception.

The ideas that drift into your mind when using the two-finger circle can make you a fortune. It pays to listen and remember. Later, write them down and daydream about them. More insight will arrive.

Your intuitive reception may not tell you the name of the horse who will win the fourth race at Churchill Downs, but it might very well tell you exactly what you need to do to double your sales.

Here is how to program or set this triggering device so that it works to amplify your spiritual messages.

ACTION PLAN

to Sensitize Intuitive Reception

1. Go in the usual way to the garden at Fairyland City.

2. Hold thumb and forefinger of the left hand (or if you are left-handed, the right hand) together to form a circle, with the other fingers extended.

3. State mentally, "Every time I hold these two fingers together I am able to concentrate easily and automatically on what a person is saying, and I can understand and remember. I am also able to listen to the intuitive messages of the universe and receive them loud and clear."

4. Leave Fairyland City in the usual way.

5. Repeat daily for several days.

6. When listening to another person, place the two fingers together.

7. When in quiet, relaxed moments, place the two fingers together, and be aware of all ideas that drift into your mind.

A FINAL TRIBUTE TO FAIRIES, ANGELS, AND OTHER HEAVENLY HOSTS

I have been rather glib in my references to angels and other celestial beings all through this book. I needed to be that way in order not to push credibility beyond any reader's limits.

Let me now remind you that there are increasing reports of help from angels coming from the general populace. A nonfiction book about angels appearing in everyday people's lives was recently on the *New York Times* bestseller list. There are newsletters about angels, catalogs about angels, conferences about angels. The *Wall Street Journal* featured a report about angels and gave it a front page position.

In the summer 1995 issue of a magazine published by the Theosophical Society called *The Quest,* two articles appeared about angels, one called "Bright Ones" by P. M. H. Atwater and the other called "Good Heavens" by Sue Diaz.

Atwater comments that angelic beings and other spiritual helpers assume their visible shape and form only for the length of time it takes to end the emergency. Then, "These angelic or light beings disappear into a featureless mass of energy or light or a radiant burst of brilliance."

A reminder might be in order that the Catholic Church and other religions teach that every person is assigned a guardian angel at birth as a guide and protector throughout life.

Could this be a case in point? A family was stranded in a snowbank when their car skidded off a seldom-used road. A man came by in a tow truck and rescued them. Once safe, the man and truck disappeared into thin air, leaving no tire tracks in the snow.

I have had angelic help with this book. I am going to take a minute to thank the heavenly host for this help. I hope you will join me.

> *Thank you, dear ones. May you in your goodness guide the readers of this book to the fulfillment of its goals.*

ONE MORE DEED THE OTHER SIDE WILL APPRECIATE

Yes, you can make this a better world to live in.

There is a way that what you are accomplishing for yourself, creating for yourself a fairy-tale life, and can change the face of the earth.

Can you create a world in which mountain streams run pure to rivers below? In which vigorous plants and animal species flourish in protected wild lands? Where people work together to preserve and pass on to future generations an environment unpolluted by their presence?

The answer is: yes, if . . .

Can you single-handedly save humankind and probably planet Earth with it from extinction?

Yes, if you share your successes with others. Teach them to daydream in a controlled way. Teach them about God's messengers in Fairyland City. Teach them to join you in living a fairy-tale life.

✌TAY IN TOUCH . . .

Designing Your Own Destiny

Guy Finley

This book is for those who are ready for a book on self-transformation with principles that actually work. *Designing Your Own Destiny* is a practical, powerful guide that tells you, in plain language, exactly what you need to do to fundamentally change yourself and your life for the better, permanently.

Eleven powerful inner life exercises will show you how to master the strong and subtle forces that actually determine your life choices and your destiny. You'll discover why so many of your daily choices up to this point have been made by default, and how embracing the truth about yourself will banish your self-defeating behaviors forever. Everything you need for spiritual success is revealed in this book. Guy Finley reveals and removes many would-be roadblocks to your inner transformation, telling you how to dismiss fear, cancel self-wrecking resentment, stop secret self-sabotage and stop blaming others for the way you feel.

After reading *Designing Your Own Destiny,* you'll understand why you are perfectly equal to every task you set for yourself, and that you truly *can* change your life for the better!

1-56718-278-X
160 pp., mass market, softcover   **$6.99**

A Rich Man's Secret

Ken Roberts

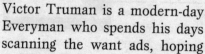

Victor Truman is a modern-day Everyman who spends his days scanning the want ads, hoping somehow to find his "right place." He has spent years reading self-help books, sitting through "get rich quick" seminars, living on unemployment checks, practicing meditation regimens, swallowing megavitamins, listening to talk radio psychologists . . . each new attempt at self-fulfillment leaving him more impoverished in spirit and wallet than he was before.

But one day, while he's retrieving an errant golf ball, Victor stumbles upon a forgotten woodland cemetery and a gravestone with the cryptic message, "Take the first step—no more, no less—and the next will be revealed." When Victor turns sleuth and discovers that this stone marks the grave of wealthy industrialist Clement Watt, whose aim was to help spiritual "orphans" find their "right place," he is compelled to follow a trail of clues that Mr. Watt seems to have left for him.

This saga crackles with the excitement of a detective story, inspires with its down-home wisdom and challenges the status quo through a penetrating look at the human comedy that Victor Truman—like all of us—is trying to understand.

1-56718-580-0
5¼ x 8, 216 pp., softcover

$9.95

To order, call 1-800-THE MOON

Prices subject to change without notice

The Llewellyn Practical Guide to Creative Visualization

Denning & Phillips

All things you will ever want must have their start in your mind. The average person uses very little of the full creative power that is his or hers, potentially. It's like the power locked in the atom—it's all there, but you have to learn to release it and apply it constructively.

If you can see it in your mind's eye, you will have it! It's true: you can have whatever you want, but there are laws to mental creation that must be followed. The power of the mind is not limited to, or limited by, the material world. Creative visualization enables humanity to reach beyond, into the invisible world of Astral and Spiritual Forces.

Through an easy series of step-by-step, progressive exercises, your mind is applied to bring desire into realization! Wealth, power, success, happiness, even psychic powers . . . even what we call magical power and spiritual attainment . . . all can be yours. You can easily develop this completely natural power, and correctly apply it for your immediate and practical benefit. Illustrated with unique, "puts-you-into-the-picture" visualization aids.

0-87542-183-0
294 pp., 5¼ x 8, illus., softcover $9.95